POEMS 1963–1983

POEMS 1963–1983

MICHAEL LONGLEY

Secker & Warburg
POETRY

Published in Great Britain 1991
by Martin Secker & Warburg Limited
Michelin House, 81 Fulham Road,
London SW3 6RB

This edition first published by the Salamander Press
and The Gallery Press 1985

A CIP catalogue record for this book
is available from the British Library
ISBN 0 436 25676 2

Designed by Michael Longley and Tom Fenton.

Set in Monotype Poliphilus roman, Blado italic and Bembo
by Speedspools, Edinburgh.
Printed in Great Britain
by St Edmundsbury Press Limited
Bury St Edmunds, Suffolk.

IN MEMORIAM
MARTIN McBIRNEY
BRIAN O'DONNELL

Stand me a last one for the road ahead,
Its roundabouts and lay-bys: no hurry when
The weather is dampening hearth and bed—
Making love in a house full of children,
Political arguments with the dead.

ACKNOWLEDGMENTS

Grateful acknowledgment is made to Macmillan & Co. Ltd, Gill & Macmillan Ltd and Dufour Editions Inc, for the poems from *No Continuing City*, and to Victor Gollancz Ltd for the poems from *An Exploded View* and *Man Lying on a Wall*.

Acknowledgments are also due to Anvil Press, Blackstaff Press and Faber & Faber for permission to print as epigraphs lines from *The Undertaking* by Louise Glück, *Stephano Remembers* by James Simmons and *Vergissmeinicht* by Keith Douglas.

Several poems from Section V, with drawings by Jim Allen, were published in 1981 by the Gallery Press in a pamphlet called *Patchwork*.

AUTHOR'S NOTE

This collection is made up of most of the poems from four volumes which are now out of print: *No Continuing City* (Macmillan, 1969), *An Exploded View* (Victor Gollancz, 1973), *Man Lying on a Wall* (Victor Gollancz, 1976) and *The Echo Gate* (Secker & Warburg, 1979). The fifth section consists of new poems. I am grateful to Kevin Crossley-Holland, my editor at Macmillan and then at Gollancz, and to Helen Owen, the poetry editor at Secker & Warburg.

Over the years I have valued publication in pamphlet form. I would like to thank Kenneth Jamison (Arts Council of Northern Ireland), Michael Emmerson (Festival Publications), Alan Tarling (Poet & Printer Press) and Harry Chambers (Phoenix Pamphlet Poets Press).

I am also very grateful to Dillon Johnston of the Wake Forest University Press in North Carolina who published *Selected Poems 1963-1980,* and to Anthony Thwaite who included a selection of my earlier work in *Penguin Modern Poets 26.*

Belfast   M.L.

The darkness lifts, imagine, in your lifetime.
Louise Glück

CONTENTS

I

No Continuing City
(1963 – 1968)

III

Man Lying on a Wall
(1972 – 1975)

IV

The Echo Gate
(1975 – 1979)

V

New Poems

I

NO CONTINUING CITY
(1963 – 1968)

for Edna

First dizzy cigarettes,
Tightlipped kisses,
Friendships, flying visits,
Birthdays, best wishes—

My children and my dead
Coming of age
In the turn of your head
As you turn a page.

For here we have no continuing city . . .

EPITHALAMION

These are the small hours when
Moths by their fatal appetite
That brings them tapping to get in,
 Are steered along the night
To where our window catches light.

 Who hazard all to be
Where we, the only two it seems,
Inhabit so delightfully
 A room it bursts its seams
And spills on to the lawn in beams,

 Such visitors as these
Reflect with eyes like frantic stars
This garden's brightest properties,
 Cruising its corridors
Of light above the folded flowers,

 Till our vicinity
Is rendered royal by their flight
Towards us, till more silently
 The silent stars ignite,
Their aeons dwindling by a night,

 And everything seems bent
On robing in this evening you
And me, all dark the element
 Our light is earnest to,
All quiet gathered round us who,

 When over the embankments
A train that's loudly reprobate
Shoots from silence into silence,
 With ease accommodate
Its pandemonium, its freight.

I hold you close because
We have decided dark will be
For ever like this and because,
    My love, already
The dark is growing elderly.

    With dawn upon its way,
Punctually and as a rule,
The small hours widening into day,
    Our room its vestibule
Before it fills all houses full,

    We too must hazard all,
Switch off the lamp without a word
For the last of night assembled
    Over it and unperturbed
By the moth that lies there littered,

    And notice how the trees
Which took on anonymity
Are again in their huge histories
    Displayed, that wherever we
Attempt, and as far as we can see,

    The flowers everywhere
Are withering, the stars dissolved,
Amalgamated in a glare,
    Which last night were revolved
Discreetly round us—and, involved,

    The two of us, in these
Which early morning has deformed,
Must hope that in new properties
    We'll find a uniform
To know each other truly by, or,

At the least, that these will,
When we rise, be seen with dawn
As remnant yet part raiment still,
   Like flags that linger on
The sky when king and queen are gone.

A QUESTIONNAIRE
FOR WALTER MITTY
for Harry Chambers

The opus virtuoso, the piano grand—
And how your unaccomplished fists extend
Themselves to musically athletic hands!

Mitty, on such voyages to legend
What luggage do you take? what currency?
Could it be truth you carry? lies you spend?

To climb an Everest or swim a sea—
No matter what the end in view—requires
A proper change of heart, some urgency.

In mixing with the doers and the triers
Whose dreaming modulates to enterprise,
Whose actions carry weight, whose churches spires,

Do you employ deceit or just disguise?
As agent, cipher or as catalyst
Do you conceal, do you apotheosise

These jungle pioneers, these pianists,
Your coinhabitants of wonderland,
Each one a namesake on the honours list?

At which side of the glass does Mitty stand
In his epiphany—in front? behind?
Or both—the hero with the also-ran?

And, Walter Mitty, how would you define
The water-walker who made the water wine—
Was it Christ the God? was it Christ the Man?

GRAFFITI

It would be painful, tedious and late
To alter awkward monsters such as these
To charming princes—metamorphoses
That all good fairy tales accelerate—

One kiss and, in the twinkling of an eye,
The Calibans accepted, warts and all,
At long last resurrected from the sty,
So blond, so beautiful, and six feet tall.

Through billboard forests, mists of lingerie,
These track a princess unequipped to change
Herself or them: her hair no winds derange,
Her thighs are locked, her cleavage legendary.

Lips where large allure but no response is,
Her all too perfect body they endure
By pencilling these bouquets of moustaches
As love's own emblem, their own signature.

Despite an aura vast enough to toss
Her neon constellations through the land,
She, in a realm too fragile to withstand
A single hair that is superfluous,

In paper palaces lies wintering,
While these who decorate her lovely crotch
With pubic shrubbery and with a notch,
Unwittingly imply a sort of spring.—

Such passion thwarted, such artistry released!
O where would Beauty be without her Beast?

EMILY DICKINSON

Emily Dickinson, I think of you
Wakening early each morning to write,
Dressing with care for the act of poetry.
Yours is always a perfect progress through
Such cluttered rooms to eloquence, delight,
To words—your window on the mystery.

In your house in Amherst Massachusetts,
Though like love letters you lock them away,
The poems are ubiquitous as dust.
You sit there writing while the light permits—
While you grow older they increase each day,
Gradual as flowers, gradual as rust.

CAMOUFLAGE

Our towns decayed, our gardens overgrown,
Weather we lament, the ivy creeping—
No matter what the setting, we are shown
(Whose one peculiar knack is weeping)
To differ from the beasts because they own
Those landscapes with which they are in keeping.

The leopard's coat accepting light through leaves,
Giraffes whose necks presume that certain trees
Are tall, whose elongated stance relieves
Those boughs of height's responsibilities—
Such attributes a balanced world conceives,
Itself reflected, its streams reflecting these.

We'd say they choose a mood to linger at:
Like white for weddings, black for funerals,
It turns to habit—then to habitat,
So deftly not a single one recalls
What he's exemplar of: more likely that
One long enlightened dawn these animals,

Betrayed by awkward mornings for an age,
By their furs and feathers long forsaken,
Put the usual scenery to advantage
But are nonetheless obliged to waken
(Amid the sanctuary of camouflage)
To a change of colour, a risk taken.

THE ORNITHOLOGICAL SECTION
in memory of John Harvey

Birds, such heavenly bric-à-bric
Without their guts, without their fears,
Despite the vital parts they lack
Have here maintained their proper cloth,
Have held their equilibrium
So perfectly, so many years,
Shed nothing but momentum,
Their only weather dust and moth.

Toward what feats and feasts they steer,
Toward what continents migrate,
Or simply why they disappear,
With feathers talons beaks and plumes
Kingfisher kestrel dodo swan
In life, in death can illustrate,
For ornithology keep on
Their uniforms, their best costumes.

In this unnatural treasury,
Though held thus by their own décors
And fixed in frozen augury,
Out of the past they dart and wade,
In such different skies to figure,
On so many half-remembered shores,
And are heading for the future,
By some deep need of ours conveyed.

Who quit their gay trajectories
Too suddenly, too long ago,
True to their movements, even these
Across our field of vision spill
And, while winging it through fable,
Fuse all we hope with what we know—
Their fate incontrovertible,
Their vanished bodies flying still.

We, with our histories left to spend,
Would have our actions thus defined
By that repose in which they end,
Would have these birds, these lively dead,
Who hesitate before they go
For ever out of sight and mind,
Whose long delays concern us so,
As our biographers instead.

We come as ornithologists—
As taxidermists we depart,
For here an urge we have persists
To recognise the tattered skins,
The bones come in at last to land
Of birds, entitled from the start,
Who take their places, make their stand
Where science ends and love begins.

THE OSPREY

To whom certain water talents—
Webbed feet, oils—do not occur,
Regulates his liquid acre
From the sky, his proper element.

There, already, his eye removes
The trout each fathom magnifies.
He lives, without compromise,
His unamphibious two lives—

An inextinguishable bird whom
No lake's waters waterlog.
He shakes his feathers like a dog.
It's all of air that ferries him.

A PERSONAL STATEMENT
for Seamus Heaney

Since you, Mind, think to diagnose
        Experience
As summer, satin, nightingale or rose,
        Of the senses making sense—
        Follow my nose,

Attend all other points of contact,
        Deserve your berth:
My brain-child, help me find my own way back
        To fire, air, water, earth.
        I am, in fact,

More than a bag of skin and bone.
        My person is
A chamber where the elements postpone
        In lively synthesis,
        In peace on loan,

Old wars of flood and earthquake, storm
        And holocaust,
Their attributes most temperately reformed
        Of heatwave and of frost.
        They take my form,

Learn from my arteries their pace—
        They leave alarms
And excursions for my heart and lungs to face.
        I hold them in my arms
        And keep in place.

To walk, to run, to leap, to stand—
Of the litany
Of movement I the vicar in command,
The prophet in my country,
The priest at hand,

Take steps to make it understood
The occupants
Assembled here in narrow neighbourhood
Are my constituents
For bad or good.

Body and Mind, I turn to you.
It's me you fit.
Whatever you think, whatever you do,
Include me in on it,
Essential Two.

Who house philosophy and force,
Wed well in me
The elements, for fever's their divorce,
Nightmare and ecstasy,
And death of course.

My sponsor, Mind, my satellite,
Keep my balance,
Steer me through my heyday, through my night,
My senses' common sense,
Selfcentred light.

And you who set me in my ways,
Immaculate,
In full possession of my faculties—
Till you disintegrate,
Exist to please.

Lest I with fears and hopes capsize,
By your own lights
Sail, Body, cargoless towards surprise.
And come, Mind, raise your sights—
Believe my eyes.

ODYSSEY

Amateur witches and professional virgins,
Sirens and shepherdesses—all new areas
Of experience (I have been out of touch)—
Ladies, you are so many and various
You will have to put up with me, for your sins,
A stranger to your islands who knows too much.

Your coy advertisements for bed and breakfast
I take as read, if I feel inclined—
So easy-going am I through going steady
(Your photographs will never hang in my mind)
With one ear cocked for the weather forecast
I come ashore to you who remind me,

And, going out of my way to take a rest,
From sea sickness and the sea recuperate,
The sad fleets of capsized skulls behind me
And the wide garden they decorate.
Grant me anchorage as your paying guest—
Landladies, I have been too long at sea.

When I sight you playing ball on the sand,
A suggestion of hair under your arms,
Or, in shallows, wearing only the waves,
I unpack strictly avuncular charms—
To lose these sea legs I walk on land:
I linger till my boat fills up with leaves,

With snow or sunshine (whichever I prefer).
I see your islands as the residue
Of my sailor days, of this life afloat,
My lonely motive to abandon you,
Darlings, after each whirlwind love affair
Becalmed in logbook and in anecdote.

You have kept me going, despite delays—
On these devious shores where we coincide
I have never once outstayed my welcome
Though you all seem last resorts, my brides—
Your faces favourite landmarks always,
Your bodies comprising the long way home.

CIRCE

The cries of the shipwrecked enter my head.
On wildest nights when the torn sky confides
Its face to the sea's cracked mirror, my bed
—Addressed by the moon and her tutored tides—

Through brainstorm, through nightmare and ocean
Keeps me afloat. Shallows are my coven,
The comfortable margins—in this notion
I stand uncorrected by the sun even.

Out of the night husband after husband
—Eyes wide as oysters, arms full of driftwood—
Wades ashore and puts in at my island.
My necklaces of sea shells and seaweed,

My skirts of spindrift, sandals of flotsam
Catch the eye of each bridegroom for ever.
Quite forgetful of the widowing calm
My sailors wait through bad and good weather.

At first in rock pools I become their wife,
Under the dunes at last they lie with me—
These are the spring and neap tides of their life.
I have helped so many sailors off the sea,

And, counting no man among my losses,
I have made of my arms and my thighs last rooms
For the irretrievable and capsized—
I extend the sea, its idioms.

NAUSICAA

You scarcely raise a finger to the tide.
Pavilions, those days off at the seaside

Collapse about your infinite arrest—
He sees your cove more clearly than the rest.

All evidence of dry land he relearns.
The ocean gathers where your shoulder turns.

NARCISSUS

Unweatherbeaten as the moon my face
Among the waterlogged, the commonplace,

Old boots and kettles for inheritance
Drifting into my head on the off-chance—

A wide Sargasso where the names of things
(Important guests at all such christenings)

Submerge in mind and pool like treasure-trove.
My face as sole survivor floats above.

My hands here, gentle, where her breasts begin,
My picture in her eyes—
It is time for me to recognise
This new dimension, my last girl.
So, to set my house in order, I imagine
Photographs, advertisements—the old lies,
The lumber of my soul—

All that is due for spring cleaning,
Everything that soul-destroys.
Into the open I bring
Girls who linger still in photostat
(For whom I was so many different boys)—
I explode their myths before it is too late,
Their promises I detonate—

There is quite a lot that I can do . . .
I leave them—are they six or seven, two or three?—
Locked in their small geographies.
The hillocks of their bodies' lovely shires
(Whose all weathers I have walked through)
Acre by acre recede entire
To summer country.

From collision to eclipse their case is closed.
Who took me by surprise
Like comets first—now, failing to ignite,
They constellate such uneventful skies,
Their stars arranged each night
In the old stories
Which I successfully have diagnosed.

Though they momentarily survive
In my delays,
They neither cancel nor improve
My continuing city with old ways,
Familiar avenues to love—
Down my one-way streets (it is time to finish)
Their eager syllables diminish.

Though they call out from the suburbs
Of experience—they know how that disturbs!—
Or, already tending towards home,
Prepare to hitch-hike on the kerbs,
Their bags full of dear untruths—
I am their medium
And I take the words out of their mouths.

From today new hoardings crowd my eyes,
Pasted over my ancient histories
Which (I must be cruel to be kind)
Only gale or cloudburst now discover,
Ripping the billboard of my mind—
Oh, there my lovers,
There my dead no longer advertise.

I transmit from the heart a closing broadcast
To my girl, my bride, my wife-to-be—
I tell her she is welcome,
Advising her to make this last,
To be sure of finding room in me
(I embody bed and breakfast)—
To eat and drink me out of house and home.

PERSEPHONE

I

I see as through a skylight in my brain
The mole strew its buildings in the rain,

The swallows turn above their broken home
And all my acres in delirium.

II

Straitjacketed by cold and numskulled
Now sleep the welladjusted and the skilled—

The bat folds its wing like a winter leaf,
The squirrel in its hollow holds aloof.

III

The weasel and ferret, the stoat and fox
Move hand in glove across the equinox.

I can tell how softly their footsteps go—
Their footsteps borrow silence from the snow.

FREEZE-UP

The freeze-up annexes the sea even,
Putting out over the waves its platform.
Let skies fall, the fox's belly cave in—
This catastrophic shortlived reform
Directs to our homes the birds of heaven.
They come on farfetched winds to keep us warm.

Bribing these with bounty, we would rather
Forget our hopes of thaw when spring will clean
The boughs, dust from our sills snow and feather,
Release to its decay and true decline
The bittern whom this different weather
Cupboarded in ice like a specimen.

THE CENTAURS

The sergeant, an arrow in his back,
Who crawled, bleeding, up the dusty street,
Who gasped his news of the failed attack,
How on all fours he made his retreat—

He put the idea into our heads.
With such horrors fixed in the mind's eye,
Saying our prayers, fingering our beads
Half awake and half asleep we lie.

Since their secret weapon is the horse
Ten thousand hooves thunder in our ears.
A nightmare! and it is getting worse—
Our hopes on foot, galloping our fears.

Hands full of reins and spurs at their feet
They herd to an awkward river bend
Our squadrons who, certain of defeat,
Are wishing they had never listened.

Into the water our youth is spilled.
We make on the causeways our last stands.
Because of the bridge we did not build
Our whole army fights for balance.

Overcome however hard we fight,
Before us all the horsemen frowning
And, no opportunities for flight,
On either side a drop to drowning.

Is our way of life pedestrian?
Can these be the customs we defend
Slow aeon after slower aeon?
But, just as we think THIS IS THE END,

We wake to a world of infantry men.
We wake from nightmare into reason—
Of their reins and bridles not a sign.
We see another sun has risen,

And, our nightmare now a mystery tour,
At ease along the river's edges
Each cavalry man become a centaur,
The causeways growing into bridges.

THE HEBRIDES
for Eavan Boland

I

The winds' enclosure, Atlantic's premises,
Last balconies
Above the waves, The Hebrides—
Too long did I postpone
Presbyterian granite and the lack of trees,
This orphaned stone

Day in, day out colliding with the sea.
Weather forecast,
Compass nor ordnance survey
Arranges my welcome
For, on my own, I have lost my way at last,
So far from home.

In whom the city is continuing,
I stop to look,
To find my feet among the ling
And bracken—over me
The bright continuum of gulls, a rook
Occasionally.

II

My eyes, slowly accepting panorama,
Try to include
In my original idea
The total effect
Of air and ocean—waterlogged all wood—
All harbours wrecked—

My dead-lights latched by whelk and barnacle
Till I abide
By the sea wall of the time I kill—
My each nostalgic scheme
Jettisoned, as crises are, the further side
Of sleep and dream.

Between wind and wave this holiday
The cormorant,
The oyster-catcher and osprey
Proceed and keep in line
While I, hands in my pockets, hesitant,
Am in two minds.

III

Old neighbours, though shipwreck's my decision,
People my brain—
Like breakwaters against the sun,
Command in silhouette
My island circumstance—my cells retain,
Perpetuate

Their crumpled deportment through bad weather.
And I feel them
Put on their raincoats for ever
And walk out in the sea.
I am, though each one waves a phantom limb,
The amputee,

For these are my sailors, these my drowned—
In their heart of hearts,
In their city I ran aground.
Along my arteries
Sluice those homewaters petroleum hurts.
Dry dock, gantries,

Dykes of apparatus educate my bones
To track the buoys
Up sea lanes love emblazons
To streets where shall conclude
My journey back from flux to poise, from poise
To attitude.

Here, at the edge of my experience,
Another tide
Along the broken shore extends
A lifetime's wrack and ruin—
No flotsam I may beachcomb now can hide
That water line.

IV

Beyond the lobster pots where plankton spreads
Porpoises turn.
Seals slip over the cockle beds.
Undertow dishevels
Seaweed in the shallows—and I discern
My sea levels.

To right and left of me there intervene
The tumbled burns—
And these, on turf and boulder weaned,
Confuse my calendar—
Their tilt is suicidal, their great return
Curricular.

No matter what repose holds shore and sky
In harmony,
From this place in the long run I,
Though here I might have been
Content with rivers where they meet the sea,
Remove upstream,

Where the salmon, risking fastest waters—
Waterfall and rock
And the effervescent otters—
On bridal pools insist
As with fin and generation they unlock
The mountain's fist.

v

Now, buttoned up, with water in my shoes,
Clouds around me,
I can, through mist that misconstrues,
Read like a palimpsest
My past—those landmarks and that scenery
I dare resist.

Into my mind's unsympathetic trough
They fade away—
And to alter my perspective
I feel in the sharp cold
Of my vantage point too high above the bay
The sea grow old.

Granting the trawlers far below their stance,
Their anchorage,
I fight all the way for balance—
In the mountain's shadow
Losing foothold, covet the privilege
Of vertigo.

A WORKING HOLIDAY
for Colin Middleton

Water through the window, the light and shade
Fill up my head once more as I distil
All that sunshine in the glass of lemonade
John left overnight on the windowsill.

And though it was the far end of my teens
I can hear him ringing bells, hear his shout—
Though my Greek's now locked in the past tense
Down the long corridors I just make out

Our classics master—'very eccentric'—
Breaking the dreams of our three weeks' stay
To get us up for breakfast and for Greek
'Because this is a working holiday.'

Into the back of my mind it all fits—
The house by the lake, Mrs Quirk
—The Keeper of the Two Colossal Tits—
Who came in to cook and do the housework.

The scholarly boy we all misunderstood,
His voice breaking, ahead of us a year,
Buck teeth champing the subjunctive mood.
His nickname was LAGOS—the Greek for HARE.

David swam naked in the pouring rain,
His foreskin like a turkey's wattle.
John's glass eye a shard of porcelain—
My comrades in the morning doing battle

With the Greek New Testament again—Acts
Of the Apostles—each of us a warden
Of views beyond our books which now contract
To Mrs Quirk by lunchtime in the garden

Gliding towards us like a huge balloon,
Behind her the water where the boat was—
The old boat which, even that afternoon,
Would be too frail to stomach all of us.

WORDS FOR JAZZ PERHAPS

for Solly Lipsitz

Elegy for Fats Waller

Lighting up, lest all our hearts should break,
His fiftieth cigarette of the day,
Happy with so many notes at his beck
And call, he sits there taking it away,
The maker of immaculate slapstick.

With music and with such precise rampage
Across the deserts of the blues a trail
He blazes, towards the one true mirage,
Enormous on a nimble-footed camel
And almost refusing to be his age.

He plays for hours on end and though there be
Oases one part water, two parts gin,
He tumbles past to reign, wise and thirsty,
At the still centre of his loud dominion—
THE SHOOK THE SHAKE THE SHEIKH OF ARABY.

Bud Freeman in Belfast

Fog horn and factory siren intercept
Each fragile hoarded-up refrain. What else
Is there to do but let those notes erupt

Until your fading last glissando settles
Among all other sounds—carefully wrapped
In the cotton wool from aspirin bottles?

To Bessie Smith

You bring from Chattanooga Tennessee
Your huge voice to the back of my mind
Where, like sea shells salvaged from the sea
As bright reminders of a few weeks' stay,
Some random notes are all I ever find.
I couldn't play your records every day.

I think of Tra/na/rossan, Inisheer,
Of Harris drenched by horizontal rain—
Those landscapes I must visit year by year.
I do not live with sounds so seasonal
Nor set up house for good. Your blues contain
Each longed/for holiday, each terminal.

To Bix Beiderbecke

In hotel rooms, in digs you went to school.
These dead were voices from the floor below
Who filled like an empty room your skull,

Who shared your perpetual one/night stand
—The havoc there, and the manœuvrings!—
Each coloured hero with his instrument.

You were bound with one original theme
To compose in your head your terminus,
Or to improvise with the best of them

That parabola from blues to barrelhouse.

IN MEMORIAM

My father, let no similes eclipse
Where crosses like some forest simplified
Sink roots into my mind; the slow sands
Of your history delay till through your eyes
I read you like a book. Before you died,
Re-enlisting with all the broken soldiers
You bent beneath your rucksack, near collapse,
In anecdote rehearsed and summarised
These words I write in memory. Let yours
And other heartbreaks play into my hands.

Now I see in close-up, in my mind's eye,
The cracked and splintered dead for pity's sake
Each dismal evening predecease the sun,
You, looking death and nightmare in the face
With your kilt, harmonica and gun,
Grow older in a flash, but none the wiser
(Who, following the wrong queue at The Palace,
Have joined the London Scottish by mistake),
Your nineteen years uncertain if and why
Belgium put the kibosh on the Kaiser.

Between the corpses and the soup canteens
You swooned away, watching your future spill.
But, as it was, your proper funeral urn
Had mercifully smashed to smithereens,
To shrapnel shards that sliced your testicle.
That instant I, your most unlikely son,
In No Man's Land was surely left for dead,
Blotted out from your far horizon.
As your voice now is locked inside my head,
I yet was held secure, waiting my turn.

Finally, that lousy war was over.
Stranded in France and in need of proof
You hunted down experimental lovers,
Persuading chorus girls and countesses:
This, father, the last confidence you spoke.
In my twentieth year your old wounds woke
As cancer. Lodging under the same roof
Death was a visitor who hung about,
Strewing the house with pills and bandages,
Till he chose to put your spirit out.

Though they overslept the sequence of events
Which ended with the ambulance outside,
You lingering in the hall, your bowels on fire,
Tears in your eyes, and all your medals spent,
I summon girls who packed at last and went
Underground with you. Their souls again on hire,
Now those lost wives as recreated brides
Take shape before me, materialise.
On the verge of light and happy legend
They lift their skirts like blinds across your eyes.

A HEADSTONE
Inscribed 'This stone claims five graves'

It told us, through the histories it lacked,
That always it grows harder to make clear
We loved, however carefully is stacked
The precious lumber that we shoulder here,
However biographical the gear:
That lives and where they end can so contract.

The sad allotment and the words we read
Owned not one date or title to undo
The silence of those people in their bed:
But someone kept like us this rendezvous—
The sinking he had launched their coffins into
Prolonged by love, till death mislaid his dead.

AFTERMATH

Imagine among these meadows
Where the soldiers sink to dust
An aftermath with swallows
Lifting blood on their breasts
Up to the homely gables, and like
A dark cross overhead the hawk.

CHRISTOPHER AT BIRTH

Your uncle, totem and curator bends
Above your cot. It is you I want to see.
Your cry comes out like an eleison.
Only the name tag round your wrist extends
My surprised compassion to loyalty.
Your mother tells me you are my godson.

The previous room still moulds your shape
Which lies unwashed, out of its element,
Smelling like rain on soil. I stoop to lift
You out of bed and into my landscape,
Last arrival, obvious immigrant
Wearing the fashions of the place you left.

As winds are balanced in a swaying tree
I cradle your cries. And in my arms reside,
Till you fall asleep, your uncontended
Demands that the world be your nursery.
And I, a spokesman of that world outside,
Creation's sponsor, stand dumbfounded,

Although there is such a story to unfold
—Whether as forecast or reminder—
Of cattle steaming in their byres, and sheep
Beneath a hedge, arranged against the cold,
Our cat at home blinking by the fender,
The wolf treading its circuits towards sleep.

THE FREEMARTIN

Comes into her own
(Her barren increments,
Her false dawn)

As excess baggage,
A currency defaced—
Quaint coinage

To farmhands, farmers
Crossing the yard
With lamps in the small hours

For such incorrigibles,
Difficult births
In byres and stables.

GATHERING MUSHROOMS

Exhaled at dawn with the cattle's breath
Out of the reticent illfitting earth,

Acre on acre the mushrooms grew—
Bonus and bounty socketed askew.

Across the fields, as though to confound
Our processions and those underground

Accumulations, secret marriages,
We drew together by easy stages.

IN A CONVENT CEMETERY

Although they've been gone for ages
On their morning walk just beyond
The icons and the cabbages,
Convening out of sight and sound
To turn slowly their missal pages,

They find us here of all places,
And I abandon to the weather
And these unlikely mistresses
Where they bed down together,
Your maidenhair, your nightdresses.

LEAVING INISHMORE

Rain and sunlight and the boat between them
Shifted whole hillsides through the afternoon—
Quiet variations on an urgent theme
Reminding me now that we left too soon
The island awash in wave and anthem.

Miles from the brimming enclave of the bay
I hear again the Atlantic's voices,
The gulls above us as we pulled away—
So munificent their final noises
These are the broadcasts from our holiday.

Oh, the crooked walkers on that tilting floor!
And the girls singing on the upper deck
Whose hair took the light like a downpour—
Interim nor change of scene shall shipwreck
Those folk on the move between shore and shore.

Summer and solstice as the seasons turn
Anchor our boat in a perfect standstill,
The harbour wall of Inishmore astern
Where the Atlantic waters overspill—
I shall name this the point of no return

Lest that excursion out of light and heat
Take on a January idiom—
Our ocean icebound when the year is hurt,
Wintertime past cure—the curriculum
Vitae of sailors and the sick at heart.

HOMAGE TO DR JOHNSON
for Philip Hobsbaum

I

The Hebridean gales mere sycophants,
So many loyal Boswells at his heel—
Yet the farflung outposts of experience
In the end undo a Roman wall,

The measured style. London is so far;
Each windswept strait he would encompass
Gives the unsinkable lexicographer
His reflection in its shattered glass.

He trudges off in the mist and the rain
Where only the thickest skin survives,
Among the rocks construes himself again,
Lifts through those altering perspectives

His downcast eyes, riding out the brainstorm,
His weatherproof enormous head at home.

II

There was no place to go but his own head
Where hard luck lodged as in an orphanage
With the desperate and the underfed.

So, surgeon himself to his dimensions,
The words still unembarrassed by their size,
He corrected death in its declensions,

The waters breaking where he stabbed the knife,
Washing his pockmarked body like a reef.

JOURNEY OUT OF ESSEX
or, *John Clare's Escape from the Madhouse*

I am lying with my head
Over the edge of the world,
Unpicking my whereabouts
Like the asylum's name
That they stitch on the sheets.

Sick now with bad weather
Or a virus from the fens,
I dissolve in a puddle
My biographies of birds
And the names of flowers.

That they may recuperate
Alongside the stunned mouse,
The hedgehog rolled in leaves,
I am putting to bed
In this rheumatic ditch

The boughs of my harvest home,
My wives, one on either side,
And keeping my head low as
A lark's nest, my feet toward
Helpston and the pole star.

RIP VAN WINKLE

You wake to find all history collapsed,
The moon in purdah and the sun eclipsed.

Turn back the newsreel of the time you killed
To the dear departed, Rip Van Winkle.

Project for us the faces of the dead,
Unlock the Sleepy Hollow of your head.

MAN FRIDAY

So much is implied on that furthest strand—
The stranger's face of course, his outstretched hand,

Houses and harbours, shillings, pence and wars,
Troy's seven layers, the canals of Mars.

To lighthouse-keepers and their like I say—
Let solitude be named Man Friday:

Our folk may muster then, even the dead,
Footprint follow footprint through my head.

BIRTHMARKS
for D.M.

You alone read every birthmark,
Only for you the tale it tells—
Idiot children in the dark
Whom we shall never bring to light,
Criminals in their prison cells—
These are the poems we cannot write.

Though we deny them name and birth,
Locked out from rhyme and lexicon
The ghosts still gather round our hearth
Whose bed and board makes up the whole—
Thief, murderer and clown—icon
And lares of the poet's soul.

II

AN EXPLODED VIEW
(1968 – 1972)

for Derek, Seamus & Jimmy

We are trying to make ourselves heard
Like the lover who mouths obscenities
In his passion, like the condemned man
Who makes a last-minute confession,
Like the child who cries out in the dark.

TO THE POETS

The dying fall, the death spasm,
Last words and catechism—

These are the ways we spend our breath,
The epitaphs we lie beneath—

Silent departures going with
The nose flute and the penis sheath.

LARES
for Raymond Warren

Farls

Cut with a cross, they are propped
Before the fire: it will take
Mug after mug of stewed tea,
Inches of butter to ease
Christ's sojourn in a broken
Oatmeal farl down your throat.

Bridget

Her rush cross over the door
Brings Bridget the cowherd home,
Milk to the dandelion,
Bread to the doorstep, the sun's
Reflection under her foot
Like a stone skimmed on water.

Furrows

My arm supporting your spine
I lay you out beneath me
Until it is your knuckles,
The small bones of foot and hand
Strewing a field where the plough
Swerves and my horses stumble.

Beds

The livestock in the yard first,
Then the cattle in the field
But especially the bees
Shall watch our eyelids lower,
Petal and sod folding back
To make our beds lazy-beds.

Neighbours

Your hand in mine as you sleep
Makes my hand a bad neighbour
Who is moving through stable
And byre, or beside the well
Stooping to skim from your milk
The cream, the dew from your fields.

Patrick

As though it were Christ's ankle
He stoops to soothe in his hand
The stone's underside: whose spine's
That ridge of first potatoes,
Whose face the duckweed spreading
On a perfect reflection.

A NATIVITY

Dog

He will be welcome to
His place in the manger,
Anaesthetist and surgeon
Muffling the child's cries
And biting through the cord
That joins God to Mary.

She-goat

A protective midwife
She roots out with her horns
A sour cake from the straw
And, jaws grinding sideways,
Devours the afterbirth
Of the child of heaven.

Bullocks

They will make a present
Of their empty purses,
Their perfected music
An interval between
The man with the scissors
And the man with the knife.

Bullfinch

Slipped in by an old master
At the edge of the picture,
An idea in Mary's head,
A splash of colour—
Thistle-tweaker, theologian,
Eater-of-thorns.

LOVE POEM

I
You define with your perfume
Infinitely shifting zones
And print in falls of talcum
The shadow of your foot.

II
Gossamers spin from your teeth,
So many light constructions
Describing as with wet wings
The gully under my tongue.

III
These wide migrations begin
In our seamier districts—
A slumdweller's pigeons
Released from creaking baskets.

CARAVAN

A rickety chimney suggests
The diminutive stove,
Children perhaps, the pots
And pans adding up to love—

So much concentrated under
The low roof, the windows
Shuttered against snow and wind,
That you would be magnified

(If you were there) by the dark,
Wearing it like an apron
And revolving in your hands
As weather in a glass dome,

The blizzard, the day beyond
And—tiny, barely in focus—
Me disappearing out of view
On probably the only horse,

Cantering off to the right
To collect the week's groceries,
Or to be gone for good
Having drawn across my eyes

Like a curtain all that light
And the snow, my history
Stiffening with the tea towels
Hung outside the door to dry.

THE ROPE-MAKERS

Sometimes you and I are like rope-makers
Twisting straw into a golden cable,
So gradual my walking backwards
You fail to notice when I reach the door,
Each step infinitesimal, a delay,
Neither a coming nor a going when
Across the lane-way I face you still
Or, at large at last in the sunny fields,
Struggle to pick you out of the darkness
Where, close to the dresser, the scrubbed table,
Fingers securing the other end, you
Watch me diminish in a square of light.

THE ADULTERER

I have laid my adulteries
Beneath the floorboards, then resettled
The linoleum so that
The pattern aligns exactly,

Or, when I bundled into the cupboard
Their loose limbs, their heads,
I papered over the door
And cut a hole for the handle.

There they sleep with their names,
My other women, their underwear
Disarranged a little,
Their wounds closing slowly.

I have watched in the same cracked cup
Each separate face dissolve,
Their dispositions
Cluster like tea leaves,

Folding a silence about my hands
Which infects the mangle,
The hearth rug, the kitchen chair
I've been meaning to get mended.

SWANS MATING

Even now I wish that you had been there
Sitting beside me on the riverbank:
The cob and his pen sailing in rhythm
Until their small heads met and the final
Heraldic moment dissolved in ripples.

This was a marriage and a baptism,
A holding of breath, nearly a drowning,
Wings spread wide for balance where he trod,
Her feathers full of water and her neck
Under the water like a bar of light.

GALAPAGOS

Now you have scattered into islands—
Breasts, belly, knees, the mount of Venus,
Each a Galapagos of the mind
Where you, the perfect stranger, prompter
Of throw-backs, of hold-ups in time,

Embody peculiar animals—
The giant tortoise hesitating,
The shy lemur, the iguana's
Slow gaze in which the *Beagle* anchors
With its homesick scientist on board.

BADGER
for Raymond Piper

I

Pushing the wedge of his body
Between cromlech and stone circle,
He excavates down mine shafts
And back into the depths of the hill.

His path straight and narrow
And not like the fox's zig-zags,
The arc of the hare who leaves
A silhouette on the sky line.

Night's silence around his shoulders,
His face lit by the moon, he
Manages the earth with his paws,
Returns underground to die.

II

An intestine taking in
patches of dog's-mercury,
brambles, the bluebell wood;
a heel revolving acorns;
a head with a price on it
brushing cuckoo-spit, goose-grass;
a name that parishes borrow.

III

For the digger, the earth-dog
It is a difficult delivery
Once the tongs take hold,

Vulnerable his pig's snout
That lifted cow-pats for beetles,
Hedgehogs for the soft meat,

His limbs dragging after them
So many stones turned over,
The trees they tilted.

THE CORNER OF THE EYE

king fisher

a knife-thrower
hurling himself, a rainbow
fractured against
the plate glass of winter:

his eye a water bead,
lens and meniscus where
the dragonfly drowns,
the water-boatman crawls.

wren

two wings criss-crossing
through gaps and loop-holes,
a mote melting towards
the corner of the eye:

or poised in the thicket
between adulteries,
small spaces circumscribed
by the tilt of his tail.

dipper

the cataract's deluge
and nightmare a curtain
he can go behind,
heavy water rolling

over feather and eye
its adhesive drops,
beneath his feet the spray
thickening into moss.

breast a warning, he
shadows the heavy-
footed earth-breakers,
bull's hoof, pheasant's toe:

is an eye that would—
if we let it in—scan
the walls for cockroaches,
for bed-bugs the beds.

CASUALTY

Its decline was gradual,
A sequence of explorations
By other animals, each
Looking for the easiest way in—

A surgical removal of the eyes,
A probing of the orifices,
Bitings down through the skin,
Through tracts where the grasses melt,

And the bad air released
In a ceremonious wounding
So slow that more and more
I wanted to get closer to it.

A candid grin, the bones
Accumulating to a diagram
Except for the polished horns,
The immaculate hooves.

And this no final reduction
For the ribs began to scatter,
The wool to move outward
As though hunger still worked there,

As though something that had followed
Fox and crow was desperate for
A last morsel and was
Other than the wind or rain.

READINGS
for Peter Longley

I

I remember your eyes in bandages
And me reading to you like a mother;
Our grubby redeemer, the chimney-sweep
Whose baptism among the seaweed
Began when he stopped astounded beside
The expensive bed, the white coverlet,
The most beautiful girl he had ever seen—
Her hair on the eiderdown like algae,
Her face a reflection in clean water;
The Irishwoman haunting Tom's shoulder—
The shawl's canopy, the red petticoats
Arriving beside him again and again,
The white feet accompanying his feet,
All of the leafy roads down to the sea.

II

Other faces at the frosty window,
Kay and Gerda in their separate attics;
The icicle driven into Kay's heart—
Then a glance at the pillow where you
Twisted your head again and tried to squeeze
Light like a tear through the bandages.

LETTERS

returning over the nightmare ground
we found the place again . . .
KEITH DOUGLAS

To Three Irish Poets

I

This, the twentieth day of March
In the first year of my middle age,
Sees me the father of a son:
Now let him in your minds sleep on
Lopsided, underprivileged
And, out of his tight burrow edged,

Your godchild while you think of him
Or, if you can't accept the term,
Don't count the damage but instead
Wet, on me, the baby's head:
About his ears our province reels
Pulsating like his fontanel,

And I, with you, when I baptise
Must calculate, must improvise
The holy water and the font,
Anything else that he may want,
And, 'priest of the muses', mock the
Malevolent *deus loci.*

II

Now that the distant islands rise
Out of the corners of my eyes
And the imagination fills
Bog-meadow and surrounding hills,
I find myself addressing you
As though I'd always wanted to:

In order to take you all in
I've had to get beneath your skin,
To colonise you like a land,
To study each distinctive hand
And, by squatter's rights, inhabit
The letters of its alphabet,

Although when I call him Daniel
(Mother and baby doing well),
Lost relations take their places,
Namesakes and receding faces:
Late travellers on the Underground
People my head like a ghost town.

III

Over the cobbles I recall
Cattle clattering to the North Wall
Till morning and the morning's rain
Rinsed out the zig-zags of the brain,
Conducting excrement and fear
Along that lethal thoroughfare:

Now every lost bedraggled field
Like a mythopoeic bog unfolds
Its gelignite and dumdums:
And should the whole idea become
A vegetable run to seed in
Even our suburban garden,

We understudy for the hare's
Disappearance around corners,
The approximate untold barks
Of the otters we call water-dogs—
A dim reflection of ourselves,
A muddy forepaw that dissolves.

IV

Blood on the kerbstones, and my mind
Dividing like a pavement,
Cracked by the weeds, by the green grass
That covers our necropolis,
The pity, terror. . . What comes next
Is a lacuna in the text,

Only blots of ink conceding
Death or blackout as a reading:
For this, his birthday, must confound
Baedekers of the nightmare ground—
And room for him beneath the hedge
With succour, school and heritage

Is made tonight when I append
Each of your names and name a friend:
For yours, then, and the child's sake
I who have heard the waters break
Claim this my country, though today
Timor mortis conturbat me.

To James Simmons

We were distracted by too many things . . .
the wine, the jokes, the music, fancy gowns.
We were no good as murderers, we were clowns.

—Who stated with the Irish queer
A preference for girls to beer—
Here's an attempt at telling all,
My confession unilateral:
Not that it matters for my part
Because I have your lines by heart,

Because the poetry you write
Is the flicker of a night-light
Picking out where it is able
Objects on the dressing table,
Glancing through the great indoors
Where love and death debate the chores,

And where, beneath a breast, you see
The blue veins in filigree,
The dust in a glass of water,
In a discarded french letter
The millions acting out their last
Collaborations with the past.

Yes, to entertain your buddies
With such transcendental studies
Rather than harmonise with hams
In yards of penitential psalms
I count among your better turns:
Play your guitar while Derry burns,

Pipe us aboard the sinking ship
Two by two. . . But before the trip
A pause, please, while the hundredth line
Squanders itself in facile rhyme—
A spry exposé of our game
But paradigmatic all the same

Like talking on as the twelfth chime
Ends nineteen hundred and ninety-nine,
The millennium and number:
For never milestones, but the camber
Dictates this journey till we tire
(So much for perning in a gyre!):

True to no 'kindred points', astride
No iridescent arc besides,
Each gives the other's lines a twist
Over supper, dinner, breakfast
To make a sort of Moebius Band,
Eternal but quotidian. . .

So, post me some octosyllabics
As redolent of death and sex
Or keep this for the rainy days
When, mindful of the final phase,
We diagnose it a relapse,
A metric following the steps

Of an ageing ballroom dancer
(Words a bow-tie round a cancer):
Or a reasonable way to move—
A Moonlight Saunter out to prove
That poetry, a tongue at play
With lip and tooth, is here to stay,

To exercise in metaphor
Our knockings at the basement door,
A ramrod mounted to invade
The vulva, Hades' palisade,
The Gates of Horn and Ivory
Or the Walls of Londonderry.

To Derek Mahon

And did we come into our own
When, minus muse and lexicon,
We traced in August sixty-nine
Our imaginary Peace Line
Around the burnt-out houses of
The Catholics we'd scarcely loved,
Two Sisyphuses come to budge
The sticks and stones of an old grudge,

Two poetic conservatives
In the city of guns and long knives,
Our ears receiving then and there
The stereophonic nightmare
Of the Shankill and the Falls,
Our matches struck on crumbling walls
To light us as we moved at last
Through the back alleys of Belfast?

Why it mattered to have you here
You who journeyed to Inisheer
With me, years back, one Easter when
With MacIntyre and the lone Dane
Our footsteps lifted up the larks,
Echoing off those western rocks
And down that darkening arcade
Hung with the failures of our trade,

Will understand. We were tongue-tied
Companions of the island's dead
In the graveyard among the dunes,
Eavesdroppers on conversations
With a Jesus who spoke Irish—
We were strangers in that parish,
Black tea with bacon and cabbage
For our sacraments and pottage,

Dank blankets making up our Lent
Till, islanders ourselves, we bent
Our knees and cut the watery sod
From the lazy-bed where slept a God
We couldn't count among our friends,
Although we'd taken in our hands
Splinters of driftwood nailed and stuck
On the rim of the Atlantic.

That was Good Friday years ago—
How persistent the undertow
Slapped by currachs ferrying stones,
Moonlight glossing the confusions
Of its each bilingual wave—yes,
We would have lingered there for less. . .
Six islanders for a ten-bob note
Rowed us out to the anchored boat.

To Seamus Heaney

From Carrigskeewaun in Killadoon
I write, although I'll see you soon,
Hoping this fortnight detonates
Your year in the United States,
Offering you by way of welcome
To the sick counties we call home
The mystical point at which I tire
Of Calor gas and a turf fire.

Till we talk again in Belfast
Pleasanter far to leave the past
Across three acres and two brooks
On holiday in a post box
Which dripping fuchsia bells surround,
Its back to the prevailing wind,
And where sanderlings from Iceland
Court the breakers, take my stand,

Disinfecting with a purer air
That small subconscious cottage where
The Irish poet slams his door
On slow-worm, toad and adder:
Beneath these racing skies it is
A tempting stance indeed—*ipsis*
Hibernicis hiberniores—
Except that we know the old stories,

The midden of cracked hurley sticks
Tied to recall the crucifix,
Of broken bones and lost scruples,
The blackened hearth, the blazing gable's
Telltale cinder where we may
Scorch our shins until that day
We sleepwalk through a No Man's Land
Lipreading to an Orange band.

Continually, therefore, we rehearse
Goodbyes to all our characters
And, since both would have it both ways,
On the oily roll of calmer seas
Launch coffin-ship and life-boat,
Body with soul thus kept afloat,
Mind open like a half-door
To the speckled hill, the plovers' shore.

So let it be the lapwing's cry
That lodges in the throat as I
Raise its alarum from the mud,
Seeking for your sake to conclude
Ulster Poet our Union Title
And prolong this sad recital
By leaving careful footprints round
A wind-encircled burial mound.

WOUNDS

Here are two pictures from my father's head—
I have kept them like secrets until now:
First, the Ulster Division at the Somme
Going over the top with 'Fuck the Pope!'
'No Surrender!': a boy about to die,
Screaming 'Give 'em one for the Shankill!'
'Wilder than Gurkhas' were my father's words
Of admiration and bewilderment.
Next comes the London-Scottish padre
Resettling kilts with his swagger-stick,
With a stylish backhand and a prayer.
Over a landscape of dead buttocks
My father followed him for fifty years.
At last, a belated casualty,
He said—lead traces flaring till they hurt—
'I am dying for King and Country, slowly.'
I touched his hand, his thin head I touched.

Now, with military honours of a kind,
With his badges, his medals like rainbows,
His spinning compass, I bury beside him
Three teenage soldiers, bellies full of
Bullets and Irish beer, their flies undone.
A packet of Woodbines I throw in,
A lucifer, the Sacred Heart of Jesus
Paralysed as heavy guns put out
The night-light in a nursery for ever;
Also a bus-conductor's uniform—
He collapsed beside his carpet-slippers
Without a murmur, shot through the head
By a shivering boy who wandered in
Before they could turn the television down
Or tidy away the supper dishes.
To the children, to a bewildered wife,
I think 'Sorry Missus' was what he said.

KINDERTOTENLIEDER

There can be no songs for dead children
Near the crazy circle of explosions,
The splintering tangent of the ricochet,

No songs for the children who have become
My unrestricted tenants, fingerprints
Everywhere, teethmarks on this and that.

THE FAIRGROUND

There, in her stall between the tattooist
And the fortune-teller, all day she sits—
The fat lady who through a megaphone
Proclaims her measurements and poundage.
Contortionists, sword-swallowers, fire-eaters

As well as a man with no arms or legs
Who rolls his own cigarettes, managing
Tobacco-pouch, paper, the box of matches
With his mouth: painstaking the performance.
He wears his woollens like a sausage-skin.

Hidden behind the broken-down equipment
Are big foreheads, bow legs, stubby fingers—
Midgets in clowns' make-up and bowler hats:
And in flowered smocks, continuously dancing,
Cretins: a carousel of tiny skulls.

Then a theatrical change in the weather
So that I am the solitary spectator:
A drenched fairground, the company advancing
And it is my head they hold in their hands.
The eyes open and close like a doll's eyes.

NIGHTMARE

In this dream I am carrying a pig,
Cradling in my arms its deceptive grin,
The comfortable folds of its baby limbs,
The feet coyly disposed like a spaniel's.

I am in charge of its delivery,
Taking it somewhere, and feeling oddly
And indissolubly attached to it—
There is nothing I can do about it,

Not even when it bites into my skull
Quite painlessly, and eats my face away,
Its juices corroding my memory,
The chamber of straight lines and purposes,

Until I am carrying everywhere
Always, on a dwindling zig-zag, the pig.

CONFESSIONS OF AN IRISH
ETHER-DRINKER

I

It freezes the puddles,
Films the tongue, its brief lozenge
Lesions of spittle and bile,
Dispersals of weather—

Icicles, bones in the ditch,
The blue sky splintering,
Water's fontanel
Closed like an eyelid.

II

My dialect becomes
Compactings of sea sounds,
The quietest drifts,
Each snowed-under
Cul-de-sac of the brain—
Glaucoma, pins and needles,
Fur on the tongue:

Or the hidden scythe
Probing farther than pain,
Its light buried in my ear,
The seed potatoes
Filling with blood—
Nuggets of darkness,
Silence's ovaries.

POTEEN

Enough running water
To cool the copper worm,
The veins at the wrist,
Vitriol to scorch the throat—

And the brimming hogshead,
Reduced by one noggin-full
Sprinkled on the ground,
Becomes an affair of

Remembered souterrains,
Sunk workshops, out-backs,
The back of the mind—
The whole bog an outhouse

Where, alongside cudgels,
Guns, the informer's ear
We have buried it—
Blood-money, treasure-trove.

Impasto or washes as a rule:
Tuberous clottings, a muddy
Accumulation, internal rhyme—
Fuchsia's droop towards the ground,
The potato and its flower:

Or a continuing drizzle,
Specialisations of light,
Bog-water stretched over sand
In small waves, elisions—
The dialects of silence:

Or, sometimes, in combination
Outlining the bent spines,
The angular limbs of creatures—
Lost minerals colouring
The initial letter, the stance.

THE ISLAND

The one saddle and bit on the island
We set aside for every second Sunday
When the priest rides slowly up from the pier.
Afterwards his boat creaks into the mist.
Or he arrives here nine times out of ten
With the doctor. They will soon be friends.

Visitors are few. A Belgian for instance
Who has told us all about the oven,
Linguists occasionally, and sociologists.
A lapsed Capuchin monk who came to stay
Was first and last to fish the lake for eels.
His carved crucifixes are still on sale.

One ship continues to rust on the rocks.
We stripped it completely of wash-hand basins,
Toilet fitments, its cargo of linoleum
And have set up house in our own fashion.
We can estimate time by the shadow
Of a doorpost inching across the floor.

In the thatch blackbirds rummaging for worms
And our dead submerged beneath the dunes.
We count ourselves historians of sorts
And chronicle all such comings and goings.
We can walk in a day around the island.
We shall reach the horizon and disappear.

THE WEST

Beneath a gas-mantle that the moths bombard,
Light that powders at a touch, dusty wings,
I listen for news through the atmospherics,
A crackle of sea-wrack, spinning driftwood,
Waves like distant traffic, news from home,

Or watch myself, as through a sandy lens,
Materialising out of the heat-shimmers
And finding my way for ever along
The path to this cottage, its windows,
Walls, sun and moon dials, home from home.

IN MEMORY OF GERARD DILLON

I

You walked, all of a sudden, through
The rickety gate which opens
To a scatter of curlews,
An acre of watery light; your grave
A dip in the dunes where sand mislays
The sound of the sea, earth over you
Like a low Irish sky; the sun
An electric light bulb clouded
By the sandy tides, sunlight lost
And found, a message in a bottle.

II

You are a room full of self-portraits,
A face that follows us everywhere;
An ear to the ground listening for
Dead brothers in layers; an eye
Taking in the beautiful predators—
Cats on the windowsill, birds of prey
And, between the diminutive fields,
A dragonfly, wings full of light
Where the road narrows to the last farm.

III

Christening robes, communion dresses,
The shawls of factory workers,
A blind drawn on the Lower Falls.

CARRIGSKEEWAUN

for Penny and David Cabot

The Mountain

This is ravens' territory, skulls, bones,
The marrow of these boulders supervised
From the upper air: I stand alone here
And seem to gather children about me,
A collection of picnic things, my voice
Filling the district as I call their names.

The Path

With my first step I dislodge the mallards
Whose necks strain over the bog to where
Kittiwakes scrape the waves: then, the circle
Widening, lapwings, curlews, snipe until
I am left with only one swan to nudge
To the far side of its gradual disdain.

The Strand

I discover, remaindered from yesterday,
Cattle tracks, a sanderling's tiny trail,
The footprints of the children and my own
Linking the dunes to the water's edge,
Reducing to sand the dry shells, the toe
And fingernail parings of the sea.

The Wall

I join all the men who have squatted here
This lichened side of the dry-stone wall
And notice how smoke from our turf fire
Recalls in the cool air above the lake
Steam from a kettle, a tablecloth and
A table she might have already set.

The Lake

Though it will duplicate at any time
The sheep and cattle that wander there,
For a few minutes every evening
Its surface seems tilted to receive
The sun perfectly, the mare and her foal,
The heron, all such special visitors.

SKARA BRAE
for Sheila and Denis Smyth

A window into the ground,
The bumpy lawn in section,
An exploded view
Through middens, through lives,

The thatch of grass roots,
The gravelly roof compounding
Periwinkles, small bones,
A calendar of meals,

The thread between sepulchre
And home a broken necklace,
Knuckles, dice scattering
At the warren's core,

Pebbles the tide washes
That conceded for so long
Living room, the hard beds,
The table made of stone.

GHOST TOWN

I have located it, my ghost town—
A place of interminable afternoons,
Sad cottages, scythes rusting in the thatch;
Of so many hesitant surrenders to
Enfolding bog, the scuts of bog cotton.

The few residents include one hermit
Persisting with a goat and two kettles
Among the bracken, a nervous spinster
In charge of the post office, a lighthouse-keeper
Who emerges to collect his groceries.

Since no one has got around to it yet
I shall restore the sign which reads CINEMA,
Rescue from the verge of invisibility
The faded stills of the last silent feature—
I shall become the local eccentric:

Already I have retired there to fill
Several gaps in my education—
The weather's ways, a handful of neglected
Pentatonic melodies and, after a while,
Dialect words for the parts of the body.

Indeed, with so much on my hands, family
And friends are definitely not welcome—
Although by the time I am accepted there
(A reputation and my own half-acre)
I shall have written another letter home.

TUTANKHAMUN

That could be me lying there
Surrounded by furniture,
My interest vested in
The persistence of objects,
An affectionate household;
The surrender of the bolt,
The wheeze of dusty hinges
Almost pleasurable
After the prolonged slumber
At my permanent address;
Cerements and substance
A sensational disclosure—
My various faces
Upside down in the spoons.

THREE POSTHUMOUS PIECES

I

In lieu of my famous last words or
The doctor's hushed diagnosis
Lifting like a draught from the door
My oracular pages, this
Will have fluttered on to the floor—
The first of my posthumous pieces.

II

As a sort of accompaniment
Drafted in different-coloured inks
Through several notebooks, this is meant
To read like a riddle from the Sphinx
And not my will and testament—
No matter what anybody thinks.

III

Two minuses become a plus
When, at the very close of play
And with the minimum of fuss,
I shall permit myself to say:
This is my Opus Posthumous—
An inspiration in its way.

ALTERA CITHERA

A change of tune, then,
On another zither,
A new aesthetic, or
The same old songs
That are out of key,
Unwashed by epic oceans
And dipped by love
In lyric waters only?

          Given under our hand
          (With a ballpoint pen)
          After the Latin of Gaius
          Sextus Propertius,
          An old friend, the shadow
          Of his former self
          Who—and this I append
          Without his permission—

Loaded the dice before
He put them in his sling
And aimed at history,
Bringing to the ground
Like lovers Caesar,
Soldiers, politicians
And all the dreary
Epics of the muscle-bound.

DOCTOR JAZZ

Hello, Central! Give me Doctor Jazz!

Jelly Roll Morton

To be nearly as great as you
Think you are, play the same tunes
Again and again: small fortunes,
Diamonds for each hollow tooth.

Django Reinhardt

A whole new method compensates
For your damaged fingers: sweat
In the creases of your forehead,
Mother-of-pearl between the frets.

King Oliver

Now all pretenders to the throne
Learn how the patient gums decay,
Music hurts: though they took away
Your bad breath, the crown's your own.

Billie Holiday

You fastened to your bony thigh
Some dollar bills and waited for
The cacophonous janitor
And silence and the cue to die.

ALIBIS

I

My botanical studies took me among
Those whom I now consider my ancestors.
I used to appear to them at odd moments—
With buckets of water in the distance, or
At the campfire, my arms full of snowy sticks.
Beech mast, hedgehogs, cresses were my diet,
My medicaments badger grease and dock leaves.
A hard life. Nevertheless, they named after me
A clover that flourished on those distant slopes.
Later I found myself playing saxophone
On the Souza Band's Grand Tour of the World.
Perhaps because so much was happening
I started, in desperation, to keep a diary.
(I have no idea what came over me.)
After that I sat near a sunny window
Waiting for pupils among the music-stands.
At present I am drafting appendices
To lost masterpieces, some of them my own—
Requiems, entertainments for popes and kings.
From time to time I choose to express myself
In this manner, the basic line. Indeed,
My one remaining ambition is to be
The last poet in Europe to find a rhyme.

II

I wanted this to be a lengthy meditation
With myself as the central character—
Official guide through the tall pavilions
Or even the saviour of damaged birds.
I accepted my responsibilities
And was managing daily after matins
And before lunch my stint of composition.
But gradually, as though I had planned it,
And with only a few more pages to go

Of my *Apologia Pro Vita Mea,*
There dawned on me this idea of myself
Clambering aboard an express train full of
Honeymoon couples and football supporters.
I had folded my life like a cheque book,
Wrapped my pyjamas around two noggins
To keep, for a while at least, my visions warm.
Tattered and footloose in my final phase
I improvised on the map of the world
And hurtled to join, among the police files,
My obstreperous bigfisted brothers.

III

I could always have kept myself to myself
And, falling asleep with the light still on,
Reached the quiet conclusion that this
(And this is where I came in) was no more than
The accommodation of different weathers,
Whirlwind tours around the scattered islands,
Telephone calls from the guilty suburbs,
From the back of the mind, a simple question
Of being in two places at the one time.

OPTIONS
for Michael Allen

Ha! here's three on's are sophisticated.
Thou art the thing itself.

These were my options: firstly
To have gone on and on—
A garrulous correspondence
Between me, the ideal reader
And—a halo to high-light
My head—that outer circle
Of critical intelligences
Deciphering—though with telling
Lacunae—my life-story,
Holding up to the bright mirrors
Of expensive libraries
My candours in palimpsest,
My collected blotting papers.

Or, at a pinch, I could have
Implied in reduced haiku
A world of suffering, swaddled
In white silence like babies
The rows of words, the mono-
Syllabic titles—my brain sore
And, as I struggled to master
The colon, my poet's tongue
Scorched by nicotine and coffee,
By the voracious acids
Of my *Ars Poetica,*
My clenched fist—towards midnight—
A paperweight on the language.

Or a species of skinny stanza
Might have materialised
In laborious versions
After the Finnish, for epigraph
The wry juxtaposing of
Wise-cracks by Groucho or Mae West
And the hushed hexameters
Of the right pastoral poet
From the Silver Age—Bacchylides
For instance—the breathings reversed,
The accents wrong mostly—proof,
If such were needed, of my humour
Among the big dictionaries.

These were my options, I say—
Night-lights, will-o'-the-wisps
Out of bog-holes and dark corners
Pointing towards the asylum
Where, for a quid of tobacco
Or a snatch of melody,
I might have cut off my head
In so many words—to borrow
A diagnosis of John Clare's—
Siphoning through the ears
Letters of the alphabet
And, with the vowels and consonants,
My life of make-believe.

AN IMAGE FROM PROPERTIUS

My head is melting,
Its cinder burnt for this:

Ankle-bone, knuckle
In the ship of death,

A load five fingers gather
Pondered by the earth.

III

MAN LYING ON A WALL
(1972 – 1975)

for Becky, Dan & Sarah

No insulation—
A house full of draughts,
Visitors, friends:

Its warmth escaping—
The snow on our roof
The first to melt.

CHECK-UP

Let this be my check-up:
Head and ear on my chest
To number the heartbeats,
Fingertips or your eyes
Taking in the wrinkles
And folds, and your body

Weighing now my long bones,
In the palm of your hand
My testicles, future:
Because if they had to
The children would eat me—
There's no such place as home.

THE LODGER

The lodger is writing a novel.
We give him the run of the house
But he occupies my mind as well—
An attic, a lumber-room
For his typewriter, notebooks,
The slowly accumulating pages.

At the end of each four-fingered
Suffering line the angelus rings—
A hundred noons and sunsets
As we lie here whispering,
Careful not to curtail our lives
Or change the names he has given us.

THE SWIM

The little rowing boat was full of
Friends and their intelligent children,
One of them bailing out for dear life
It seemed, while with an indolent hand

Another trailed a V on the lake
And directed it towards the island
Like an arrow. And nobody looked
As we undressed quickly and jumped in.

All of you vanished except your head:
Shoulders dissolving, and your arms too,
So opaque the element which could,
I knew, bend a stick at the elbow

Or, taking the legs from under you,
In its cat's-cradle of cross-currents
Like a bridegroom lift you bodily
Over the threshold to the island.

To risk brambles and nettles because
We wanted to make love there and then
In spite of the mud between my toes,
The weeds showing like veins on your skin,

Did seem all that remained to be done
As the creak of the rowlocks faded
And our friends left us to be alone
Or whatever they had decided.

THE GOOSE

Remember the white goose in my arms,
A present still. I plucked the long
Flight-feathers, down from the breast,
Finest fuzz from underneath the wings.

I thought of you through the operation
And covered the unmolested head,
The pink eyes that had persisted in
An expression of disappointment.

It was right to hesitate before
I punctured the skin, made incisions
And broached with my reluctant fingers
The chill of its intestines, because

Surviving there, lodged in its tract,
Nudging the bruise of the orifice
Was the last egg. I delivered it
Like clean bone, a seamless cranium.

Much else followed which, for your sake,
I bundled away, burned on the fire
With the head, the feet, the perfect wings.
The goose was ready for the oven.

I would boil the egg for your breakfast,
Conserve for weeks the delicate fats
As in the old days. In the meantime
We dismantled it, limb by limb.

DREAMS

I

Your face with hair
Falling over it
Was all of your mind
That I understood,

At the bottom of which
Like a windfall
I lay and waited
For your eyes to open.

II

I am a hot head
That quits the pillow,
A pair of feet
Numb with nightmare

Near the chilly lake
Of faithful swans
Or the clean mating
Of wolves in the snow.

LOVE POEM

If my nose could smell only
You and what you are about,
If my fingertips, tongue, mouth
Could trace your magnetic lines,
Your longitudes, latitudes,
If my eyes could see no more
Than dust accumulating
Under your hair, your skin's
Removals and departures,
The glacial progression
Of your fingernails, toenails,
If my ears could hear nothing
But the noise of your body's
Independent processes,
Lungs, heartbeat, intestines,
Then I would be lulled in sleep
That soothes for a lifetime
The scabby knees of boyhood,
And alters the slow descent
Of the scrotum towards death.

BELLADONNA

I

Mischievous berries release the drug
That whitens her complexion and makes
Black pools of the pupils of her eyes,
Her face reflecting my face, eyelids
A sparrow watering its wings there
Or a butterfly drowned in the cup.

II

I have surrounded her with bottles
—Whiskey, medicines, assorted drugs—
I am a drunk, an addict, and she
The genie behind the glass, released
When I drink at her mouth, when I smell
Through her nostrils these substances.

III

She and I are blood donors, prepared
As specimens for the microscope,
Transparencies of Christ's example
And, as anybody's future now,
Strangers, our identities smothered
Under the wing of the pelican.

Though there are distances between us
I lean across and with my finger
Pick sleep from the corners of her eyes,
Two grains of sand. Could any soldier
Conscripted to such desert warfare
Discern more accurately than I do
The numerous hazards—a high sun,
Repetitive dunes, compasses jamming,
Delirium, death—or dare with me
During the lulls in each bombardment
To address her presence, her absence?
She might be a mirage, and my long
Soliloquies part of the action.

IN MAYO

I

For her sake once again I disinter
Imagination like a brittle skull
From where the separating vertebrae
And scapulae litter a sandy wind,

As though to reach her I must circle
This burial mound, its shadow turning
Under the shadow of a seabird's wing:
A sundial for the unhallowed soul.

II

Though the townland's all ears, all eyes
To decipher our movements, she and I
Appear on the scene at the oddest times:
We follow the footprints of animals,

Then vanish into the old wives' tales
Leaving behind us landmarks to be named
After our episodes, and the mushrooms
That cluster where we happen to lie.

III

When it is time for her to fall asleep
And I touch her eyelids, may night itself,
By my rule of thumb, be no profounder
Than the grassy well among irises

Where wild duck shelter their candid eggs:
No more beguiling than a gull's feather
In whose manifold gradations of light
I clothe her now and erase the scene.

IV

Dawns and dusks here should consist of
Me scooping a hollow for her hip-bone,
The stony headland a bullaun, a cup
To balance her body in like water:

Then a slow awakening to the swans
That fly home in twos, married for life,
Larks nestling beside the cattle's feet
And snipe the weight of the human soul.

WEATHER

I carry indoors
Two circles of blue sky,
Splinters of sunlight
As spring water tilts
And my buckets, heavy

Under the pressure of
Enormous atmospheres,
Two lakes and the islands
Enlarging constantly,
Tug at my shoulders, or,

With a wet sky low as
The ceiling, I shelter
Landmarks, keep track of
Animals, all the birds
In a reduced outdoors

And open my windows,
The wings of dragonflies
Hung from an alder cone,
A raindrop enclosing
Brookweed's five petals.

FLORA

A flutter of leaves
And pages open
Where, as my bookmark,
A flower is pressed,

Calyx, filament,
Anther staining
These pictures of me
In waste places

Shadowing sheep-tracks
From seacliff to dunes,
Ditches that drain
The salty marshes,

Naming the outcasts
Where petal and bud
Colour a runnel
Or sodden pasture,

Where bell and bugle,
A starry cluster
Or butterfly wing
Convey me farther

And in memory
And hands deposit
Blue periwinkles,
Meadowsweet, tansy.

POINTS OF THE COMPASS
for John Hewitt

Inscription

A stone inscribed with a cross,
The four points of the compass
Or a confluence of lines,
Crossroads and roundabout:
Someone's last milestone, propped
At an angle to the nettles,
A station that staggers still
Through tendrils of silverweed:
To understand what it says
I have cleared this area
Next to the casual arc
A thorn traces upon stone.

Clapper Bridge

One way to proceed:
Taking the water step
By step, stepping stones
With a roof over them,
A bed of standing stones,
Watery windows sunk
Into a dry-stone wall,
Porches for the water,
Some twists completing it
And these imperfections
Set, like the weather,
On the eve of mending.

Cell

After the entire structure
Has been sited thoughtfully
To straddle a mountain stream,
The ideal plan would include
A path leading from woodland,
From sorrel and watercress
To the one door, a window
Framing the salmon weir,
A hole for smoke, crevices
For beetles or saxifrage
And, for the fear of flooding,
Room enough under the floor.

Standing Stone

Where two lakes suggest petals
Of vetch or the violet,
The wings of a butterfly,
Ink blots reflecting the mind,
There, to keep them apart
As versions of each other,
To record the distances
Between islands of sunlight
And, as hub of the breezes,
To administer the scene
From its own peninsula,
A stone stands, a standing stone.

FLEADH
for Brian O'Donnell

Fiddle

Stained with blood from a hare,
Then polished with beeswax
It suggests the vibration
Of diaphanous wings
Or—bow, elbow dancing—
Follows the melted spoors
Where fast heels have spun
Dewdrops in catherine-wheels.

Flute

Its ebony and silver
Mirror a living room
Where disembodied fingers
Betray to the darkness
Crevices, every knothole—
Hearth and chimney-corner
For breezes igniting
The last stick of winter.

Bodhran

We have eaten the goat:
Now his discarded horns
From some farflung midden
Call to his skin, and echo
All weathers that rattle
The windows, bang the door:
A storm contained, hailstones
Melting on this diaphragm.

Whistle

Cupped hands unfolding
A flutter of small wings
And fingers a diamond
Would be too heavy for,
Like ice that snares the feet
Of such dawn choruses
And prevents the robin
Ripening on its branch.

Pipes

One stool for the fireside
And the field, for windbag
And udder: milk and rain
Singing into a bucket
At the same angle: cries
Of waterbirds homing:
Ripples and undertow—
The chanter, the drones.

LANDSCAPE

Here my imagination
Tangles through a turfstack
Like skeins of sheep's wool:
Is a bull's horn silting
With powdery seashells.

I am clothed, unclothed
By racing cloud shadows,
Or else disintegrate
Like a hillside neighbour
Erased by sea mist.

A place of dispersals
Where the wind fractures
Flight-feathers, insect wings
And rips thought to tatters
Like a fuchsia petal.

For seconds, dawn or dusk,
The sun's at an angle
To read inscriptions by:
The splay of the badger
And the otter's skidmarks

Melting into water
Where a minnow flashes:
A mouth drawn to a mouth
Digests the glass between
Me and my reflection.

FURY

On his mother's flank
A twist of blood, straw
Trailing to his crib
Behind the milk churns,

In the high rafters
Martins that chatter
Above his silence,
The white of his eye,

His enormous head's
Dithering acceptance
Of a breach birth,
A difficult name.

Somewhere already
The hiss of scythes,
The forking of hay
For his bony frame,

Over laid grasses
And thistles crows
Hustling to pin down
The new evictions.

I can just make out
His starry forehead
Hesitant among
Eyebright and speedwell.

TRUE STORIES
for Rebecca and Daniel

The Ring

I was ferried out to where
Petrels flung from the cliff face
Their long bodies, and underfoot
Plovers piled on pebbles
More pebbles, speckled eggs,

Four segments to each circle
Which I half-inscribed for you
By echoing both your names
And by fastening my ring
Around a fledgling's leg.

The Egg
for Daniel

It was your birth over again
Happening in my head as I let
Unfold in the palm of my hand
A tiny squeaking, a skull, feet,
Wings that the shell had compressed,

Yours the fulmar's exquisite eye
Balancing above one clean egg
And taking in all of the island,
The solitary snow goose, whiteness,
Bird lime among the sea campions.

The Nest

Next door to the tussocky well
I uncovered the lark's snug nest,
Our orderly neighbour: enough
To occupy you while you slept
Warming the eggs and silencing

The mallard's waterlogged alarum
From the bog, who, to spite the heron
And deflect a dangerous sky,
Had fouled her nest before leaving
And stained the immaculate shells.

The Wren
for Rebecca

After your two nightmares
(One about a giant bird
Lowering itself from the sky:
In the other both your eyes
Grew featureless as eggshells)

You were first to discover
A wren trapped in the kitchen:
Two pulses fluttering until
You had opened the window
On broken dreams, true stories.

FERRY

I loop around this bollard
The beeline of cormorants,
The diver's shifts in air
And secure my idea
Of the island: rigging

Slanted across the sky,
Then a netting of sunlight
Where the thin oar splashes,
Stone steps down to the water
And a forgotten ferry.

HALCYON

Grandmother's plumage was death
To the few remaining grebes,
The solitary kingfisher
That haunted a riverbank.

But, then, I consider her
The last of the Pearly Queens
To walk under tall feathers—
The trophies of sweethearts

Who aimed from leafy towpaths
Pistols, silver bullets,
Or sank among bullrushes
Laying out nets of silk.

So many trigger fingers
And hands laid upon water
Should let materialise
A bird that breeds in winter,

That settles bad weather,
The winds of sickness and death—
Halcyon to the ancients
And kingfisher in those days,

Though perhaps even she knew
It was the eccentric grebe
Whose feet covered the surface,
Whose nest floated on the waves.

STILTS
for Paul Muldoon

Two grandfathers sway on stilts
Past my bedroom window.
They should be mending holes
In the Big Top, but that would be
Like putting out the stars.

The first has been a teacher
Of ballroom dancing, but now
Abandons house and home
To lift in the Grand Parade
High knees above the neighbours.

The second, a carpenter,
Comes from another town
With tools and material
To manufacture stilts
And playthings for the soul.

MASTER OF CEREMONIES

My grandfather, a natural master of ceremonies
('Boys! Girls! Take your partners for the Military Two-step!')
Had thrown out his only son, my sad retarded uncle
Who, good for nothing except sleepwalking to the Great War,
Was not once entrusted with a rifle, bayonet but instead
Went over the top slowly behind the stretcher parties
And, as park attendant where all hell had broken loose,
Collected littered limbs until his sack was heavy.
In old age my grandfather demoted his flesh and blood
And over the cribbage board ('Fifteen two, fifteen four,
One for his nob') would call me Lionel. 'Sorry. My mistake.
That was my nephew. His head got blown off in No Man's Land.'

EDWARD THOMAS'S WAR DIARY

1 January – 8 April, 1917

One night in the trenches
You dreamed you were at home
And couldn't stay to tea,
Then woke where shell holes
Filled with bloodstained water,

Where empty beer bottles
Littered the barbed wire—still
Wondering why there sang
No thrushes in all that
Hazel, ash and dogwood,

Your eye on what remained—
Light spangling through a hole
In the cathedral wall
And the little conical
Summer house among trees.

Green feathers of yarrow
Were just fledging the sods
Of your dugout when you
Skirted the danger zone
To draw panoramas,

To receive larks singing
Like a letter from home
Posted in No Man's Land
Where one frantic bat seemed
A piece of burnt paper.

MOLE

Does a mole ever get hit by a shell?
EDWARD THOMAS in his diary, 25.2.17

Who bothers to record
This body digested
By its own saliva
Inside the earth's mouth
And long intestine,

Or thanks it for digging
Its own grave, darkness
Growing like an eyelid
Over the eyes, hands
Swimming in the soil?

FLEANCE

I entered with a torch before me
And cast my shadow on the backcloth
Momentarily: a handful of words,
One bullet with my initials on it—
And that got stuck in a property tree.

I would have caught it between my teeth
Or, a true professional, stood still
While the two poetic murderers
Pinned my silhouette to history
In a shower of accurate daggers.

But as any illusionist might
Unfasten the big sack of darkness,
The ropes and handcuffs, and emerge
Smoking a nonchalant cigarette,
I escaped—only to lose myself.

It took me a lifetime to explore
The dusty warren beneath the stage
With its trapdoor opening on to
All that had happened above my head
Like noises off or distant weather.

In the empty auditorium I bowed
To one preoccupied caretaker
And, without removing my make up,
Hurried back to the digs where Banquo
Sat up late with a hole in his head.

MAN LYING ON A WALL
Homage to L. S. Lowry

You could draw a straight line from the heels,
Through calves, buttocks and shoulderblades
To the back of the head: pressure points
That bear the enormous weight of the sky.
Should you take away the supporting structure
The result would be a miracle or
An extremely clever conjuring trick.
As it is, the man lying on the wall
Is wearing the serious expression
Of popes and kings in their final slumber,
His deportment not dissimilar to
Their stiff, reluctant exits from this world
Above the shoulders of the multitude.

It is difficult to judge whether or not
He is sleeping or merely disinclined
To arrive punctually at the office
Or to return home in time for his tea.
He is wearing a pinstripe suit, black shoes
And a bowler hat: on the pavement
Below him, like a relic or something
He is trying to forget, his briefcase
With everybody's initials on it.

ARS POETICA

I

Because they are somewhere in the building
I'll get in touch with them, the wife and kids—
Or I'm probably a widower by now,
Divorced and here by choice, on holiday
And paying through the nose for it: a queue
Of one outside the bathroom for ever
And no windows with a view of the sea.

II

I am writing a poem at the office desk
Or else I am forging business letters—
What I am really up to, I suspect,
Is seducing the boss's secretary
Among the ashtrays on the boardroom table
Before absconding with the petty-cash box
And a one-way ticket to Katmandu.

III

I go disguised as myself, my own beard
Changed by this multitude of distortions
To stage whiskers, my hair a give-away,
A cheap wig, and my face a mask only—
So that, on entering the hall of mirrors
The judge will at once award the first prize
To me and to all of my characters.

IV

After I've flown my rickety bi-plane
Under the Arc de Triomphe and before
I perform a double back-somersault
Without the safety net and—if there's time—
Walk the high wire between two waterfalls,
I shall draw a perfect circle free-hand
And risk my life in a final gesture.

V

Someone keeps banging the side of my head
Who is well aware that it's his furore,
His fists and feet I most want to describe—
My silence to date neither invitation
Nor complaint, but a stammering attempt
Once and for all to get him down in words
And allow him to push an open door.

VI

I am on general release now, having
Put myself in the shoes of all husbands,
Dissipated my substance in the parlours
Of an entire generation and annexed
To my territory gardens, allotments
And the desire—even at this late stage—
To go along with the world and his wife.

COMPANY

I imagine a day when the children
Are drawers full of soft toys, photographs
Beside the only surviving copies
Of the books that summarise my lifetime,
And I have begun to look forward to
Retirement, second childhood, except that
Love has diminished to one high room
Below which the vigilantes patrol
While I attempt to make myself heard
Above the cacophonous plumbing, and you
Who are my solitary interpreter
Can bear my company for long enough
To lipread such fictions as I believe
Will placate remote customs officials,
The border guards, or even reassure
Anxious butchers, greengrocers, tradesmen
On whom we depend for our daily bread,
The dissemination of manuscripts,
News from the outside world, simple acts
Of such unpatriotic generosity
That until death we hesitate together
On the verge of an almost total silence:

Or else we are living in the country
In a far-off townland divided by
The distances it takes to overhear
A quarrel or the sounds of love-making,
Where even impoverished households
Can afford to focus binoculars
On our tiny windows, the curtains
That wear my motionless silhouette
As I sit late beside a tilley-lamp
And try to put their district on the map
And to name the fields for them, for you
Who busy yourself about the cottage,

Its thatch letting in, the tall grasses
And the rain leaning against the half-door,
Dust on the rafters and our collection
Of curious utensils, pots and pans
The only escape from which is the twice
Daily embarrassed journey to and from
The well we have choked with alder branches
For the cattle's safety, their hoofprints
A thirsty circle in the puddles,
Watermarks under all that we say.

LAST RITES

I

I keep my own death-watch:
Mine the disembodied eye
At the hole in my head,
That blinks, watches through
Judas-hatch, fontanel:

Thus, round the clock, the last
Rites again and again:
A chipped mug, a tin plate
And no one there but myself,
My own worst enemy.

II

They can put out the drag-net:
Squads of intelligent detectives
Won't discover the hairs of my beard
Lodged like bookmarks between the pages
In even the remotest library,

Or the hairs of my head unravelling
For some Ariadne along dark
Corridors and back into my head,
Or the truth of my body, its sperm
Outnumbering the women in the world.

IV

THE ECHO GATE
(1975 – 1979)

for Michael Allen & Paul Muldoon

> *I have heard of an island*
> *With only one house on it.*
> *The gulls are at home there.*
> *Our perpetual absence*
> *Is a way of leaving*
> *All the eggs unbroken*
> *That litter the ground*
> *Right up to its doorstep.*

OBSEQUIES

They are proof-reading my obituary now
As I fall asleep in formalin and float
Just below the surface of death, mute
At the centre of my long obsequies.

Were they to queue up to hear me breathing
The chemicals, then head over heels
All my lovers would fall in love again,
For I am a big fish in the aquarium,

A saint whose bits and pieces separate
Into a dozen ceremonies, pyres
For hands that bedded down like Gandhi
With the untouchables, funerals for feet.

They have set my eyes like two diamonds
In the black velvet of another's head,
Bartered silver, gold from knuckle and tooth
To purchase some sustenance for the needy.

Meanwhile, back at the dissecting theatre,
Part of me waits to find in sinks and basins
A final ocean, tears, water from the tap,
Superstitious rivers to take me there.

OLIVER PLUNKETT

His Soul

When they cut off his head, the long whiskers
Went on growing, as if to fledge his soul
And facilitate its gradual departure.

So much of him was concentrated there
That, quite without his realizing it,
They divided the body into four.

It amounted to more than a withdrawal
When the last drop of moisture had dispersed
And one by one the hairs fell from his chin,

For the fatty brain was shrivelling as well,
Leaving around itself enormous spaces
And accommodation for the likes of him.

His own leathery shrine, he seems to be
Refracting the gleam in his father's eye
Like a shattered mirror in a handbag.

His Head

This is the end of the body that thinks
And says things, says things as the body does—
Kisses, belches, sighs—while making room for
The words of wisdom and the testimonies.

And these are a baby's features, a child's
Expression condensing on the plate glass,
The specimen suspended in its bottle
At eye level between shelf and shelf.

His head looks out from the tiny coffin
As though his body were crouching there
Inside the altar, a magician
Who is in charge of this conjuring trick,

Or an astronaut trapped by his oxygen
And eager to float upwards to the ceiling
Away from the gravitational pull
Of his arms and legs which are very old.

Your own face is reflected by the casket
And this is anybody's head in a room
Except that the walls are all windows and
He has written his name over the glass.

His Body

Trying to estimate what height he was
Keeps the soul awake, like the pea under
The heap of mattresses under the princess.

And now that they've turned him into a saint
Even a fly buzzing about the roof space
Must affect the balance of his mind.

His thigh bones and shoulder blades are scales
That a speck of dust could tilt, making him
Walk with a limp or become a hunchback.

He has been buried under the fingernails
Of his executioners, until they too fade
Like the lightning flash of their instruments.

There accompanies him around the cathedral
Enough silence to register the noise
Of the hairs on arms and legs expiring.

WREATHS

The Civil Servant

He was preparing an Ulster fry for breakfast
When someone walked into the kitchen and shot him:
A bullet entered his mouth and pierced his skull,
The books he had read, the music he could play.

He lay in his dressing gown and pyjamas
While they dusted the dresser for fingerprints
And then shuffled backwards across the garden
With notebooks, cameras and measuring tapes.

They rolled him up like a red carpet and left
Only a bullet hole in the cutlery drawer:
Later his widow took a hammer and chisel
And removed the black keys from his piano.

The Greengrocer

He ran a good shop, and he died
Serving even the death-dealers
Who found him busy as usual
Behind the counter, organised
With holly wreaths for Christmas,
Fir trees on the pavement outside.

Astrologers or three wise men
Who may shortly be setting out
For a small house up the Shankill
Or the Falls, should pause on their way
To buy gifts at Jim Gibson's shop,
Dates and chestnuts and tangerines.

Christ's teeth ascended with him into heaven:
Through a cavity in one of his molars
The wind whistles: he is fastened for ever
By his exposed canines to a wintry sky.

I am blinded by the blaze of that smile
And by the memory of my father's false teeth
Brimming in their tumbler: they wore bubbles
And, outside of his body, a deadly grin.

When they massacred the ten linen workers
There fell on the road beside them spectacles,
Wallets, small change, and a set of dentures:
Blood, food particles, the bread, the wine.

Before I can bury my father once again
I must polish the spectacles, balance them
Upon his nose, fill his pockets with money
And into his dead mouth slip the set of teeth.

LAST REQUESTS

I

Your batman thought you were buried alive,
Left you for dead and stole your pocket watch
And cigarette case, all he could salvage
From the grave you so nearly had to share
With an unexploded shell. But your lungs
Surfaced to take a long remembered drag,
Heart contradicting as an epitaph
The two initials you had scratched on gold.

II

I thought you blew a kiss before you died,
But the bony fingers that waved to and fro
Were asking for a Woodbine, the last request
Of many soldiers in your company,
The brand you chose to smoke for forty years
Thoughtfully, each one like a sacrament.
I who brought peppermints and grapes only
Couldn't reach you through the oxygen tent.

SECOND SIGHT

My father's mother had the second sight.
Flanders began at the kitchen window—
The mangle rusting in No Man's Land, gas
Turning the antimacassars yellow
When it blew the wrong way from the salient.

In bandages, on crutches, reaching home
Before his letters, my father used to find
The front door on the latch, his bed airing.
'I watched my son going over the top.
He was carrying flowers out of the smoke.'

I have brought the *Pocket Guide to London,*
My *Map of the Underground,* an address—
A lover looking for somewhere to live,
A ghost among ghosts of aunts and uncles
Who crowd around me to give directions.

Where is my father's house, where my father?
If I could walk in on my grandmother
She'd see right through me and the hallway
And the miles of cloud and sky to Ireland.
'You have crossed the water to visit me.'

HOME GROUND

I
for S.H.

This was your home ground, comings and goings
When the sand martins collected in flight
Feathers and straw for untidy chambers
Or swooped up to kiss each tiny darkness,
Five white eggs changing to five white chins:

Childhood, and your townland poor enough
For gentians, fairy-flax, wild strawberries
And the anxious lapwing that settled there,
Its vocal chords a grass blade stretched
Between your thumbs and blown to tatters.

II
for P.M.

When they landed the first man on the moon
You were picking strawberries in a field,
Straggly fuses, lamps that stained the ground
And lips and fingers with reflected light,
For you were living then from hand to mouth.

Re-entering that atmosphere, you take
The dangerous bend outside the graveyard
Where your mother falls like a meteor
From clouds of may and damson blossom:
There the moon-rocks ripen in your hand.

ARCHITECTURE

The House on the Seashore

Laying down sand and shingle for the floor
And thatching with seaweed the low boulders
You make an echo-chamber of your home
That magnifies the wind to a cyclone
And keeps you from standing head and shoulders
Above the sea's whisper and the seashore.

The House Shaped Like an Egg

Do you pay for this house with egg money
Since its whitewashed walls are clean as shell
And the parlour, scullery, bedrooms oval
To leave no corner for dust or devil
Or the double yolk of heaven and hell
Or days when it rains and turns out sunny?

The House on the Bleach Green

This stump of a tree without any leaves
Can be occupied but never lived in
When snow is lying on the bleach green
And the smallest house you have ever seen
Lets someone inside to watch the linen
From tiny windows with a view of thieves.

The House Made out of Turf

Are the hearth and the chimney built of stone
Or can there be a fireplace for the fire
In a house made out of turf, with its roof
Of kindling, gables that may waterproof
This spacious tinderbox to make a pyre
Of what you built and heated on your own?

153

ASH KEYS

Ghosts of hedgers and ditchers,
The ash trees rattling keys
Above tangles of hawthorn
And bramble, alder and gorse,

Would keep me from pacing
Commonage, long perspectives
And conversations, a field
That touches the horizon.

I am herding cattle there
As a boy, as the old man
Following in his footsteps
Who begins the task again,

As though there'd never been
In some interim or hollow
Wives and children, milk
And buttermilk, market days.

Far from the perimeter
Of watercress and berries,
In the middle of the field
I stand talking to myself,

While the ash keys scatter
And the gates creak open
And the barbed wire rusts
To hay-ropes strung with thorns.

FROZEN RAIN

I slow down the waterfall to a chandelier,
Filaments of daylight, bones fleshed out by ice
That recuperate in their bandages of glass
And, where the lake behaves like a spirit-level,
I save pockets of air for the otter to breathe.

I magnify each individual blade of grass
With frozen rain, a crop of icicles and twigs,
Fingers and thumbs that beckon towards the thaw
And melt to the marrow between lip and tongue
While the wind strikes the branches like a celeste.

THAW

Snow curls into the coalhouse, flecks the coal.
We burn the snow as well in bad weather
As though to spring-clean that darkening hole.
The thaw's a blackbird with one white feather.

SPRING TIDE

I

I seem lower than the distant waves,
Their roar diluting to the stillness
Of the sea's progression across these flats,
A map of water so adjusted
It behaves like a preservative
And erases neither the cattle's
And the sheep's nor my own footprints.
I leave hieroglyphics under glass
As well as feathers that hardly budge,
Down abandoned at preening places
That last so long as grassy islands
Where swans unravel among the ferns.

II

It isn't really a burial mound
Reflected there, but all that remains
Of a sandy meadow, a graveyard
Where it was easy to dig the graves.
The spring tide circles and excavates
A shrunken ramshackle pyramid
Rinsing cleaner scapulae, tibias,
Loose teeth, cowrie and nautilus shells
Before seeping after sun and moon
To pour cupfuls into the larks' nests,
To break a mirror on the grazing
And lift minnows over the low bridge.

The spring tide has ferried jelly fish
To the end of the lane, pinks, purples,
Wet flowers beside the floating cow-pats.
The zig-zags I make take me among
White cresses and brookweed, lousewort,
Water plantain and grass of parnassus
With engraved capillaries, ivory sheen:
By a dry-stone wall in the dune slack
The greenish sepals, the hidden blush
And a lip's red veins and yellow spots—
Marsh helleborine waiting for me
To come and go with the spring tide.

LORE

Cutting the Last Sheaf

Divide into three braids the thickest clump of corn
Plaiting it like hair, tying it below the ears
To make sure that the harvest will not unravel,

Then, as though to hone them sharper upon the wind
Throw sickles until the last sheaf has been severed
And give it to a woman or a mare in foal.

Fishing for Sand Eels

They are hungry enough to fish for eels,
Sand eels, except that it's hardly fishing
To parade so slowly between the tides,

To be one of the moonlit multitude,
To slice sand and sea with a blunt sickle
Lest the harvest bleed when it is cut.

Working the Womenfolk

The man who would like his wife to dig in the fields
Will have to attach a wooden peg to her hoe,
Then cover her feet, and not with stockings only,

And do his bit at the milking stool and the churn
And even keep an eye on the wandering hen
For fear she might be laying in the nettle patch.

Bringing in the Kelp

There are even more fields under the sea
As though waves washed over a remote farm
And lanes extended there for cart or raft,

As though the handles of rake and sickle
Grew much longer in order to harvest
The salty tangle from those deep waters.

Ploughing by the Tail

Whoever plucks wool in thrifty skeins from his sheep
And bleeds his bull through a small hole in the neck
And blows into his cow to make her give more milk,

Is likely to do without a halter and reins
And plough by the tail, if the hairs are strong enough
And he has learned to tie the complicated knot.

Finding a Remedy

Sprinkle the dust from a mushroom or chew
The white end of a rush, apply the juice
From fern roots, stems of burdock, dandelions,

Then cover the wound with cuckoo-sorrel
Or sphagnum moss, bringing together verse
And herb, plant and prayer to stop the bleeding.

THE ECHO GATE

I stand between the pillars of the gate,
A skull between two ears that reconstructs
Broken voices, broken stones, history

And the first words that come into my head
Echoing back from the monastery wall
To measure these fields at the speed of sound.

ON HEARING IRISH SPOKEN

Gliding together in a tidal shimmer to talk
Two fishermen leave behind another currach
Upturned on the beach, a hand cupped to an ear,

An echo of technical terms, the one I know
Repeating itself at desperate intervals
Like the stepping stones across a river in spate.

MAYO MONOLOGUES

Brothers

I was a mother and a father to him
Once his pebble spectacles had turned cloudy
And his walk slowed to a chair by the fire.
Often I would come back from herding sheep
Or from the post office with our pensions
To find his darkness in darkness, the turf
Shifting ashes on to last flakes of light.
The room was made more silent by the flies
That circled the soup stains on his waistcoat.
The dog preferred to curl up under his hand
And raced ahead as soon as I neared the lane.
I read to him from one of his six books,
Thick pages dropping from the broken spines
Of *Westward Ho!* and *The Children's Reciter.*
Sometimes I pulled faces, and he didn't know,
Or I paraded naked in front of him
As though I was looking in a mirror.
Two neighbours came visiting after he died.
Mad for the learning, a character, they said
And awakened in me a pride of sorts.
I picture his hand when I stroke the dog,
His legs if I knock the kettle from the hearth.
It's his peculiar way of putting things
That fills in the spaces of Tullabaun.
The dregs stewed in the teapot remind me,
And wind creaming rainwater off the butt.

She burst out laughing at the interview
Because he complained about his catheter.
I had come from the far end of the county
To nurse his lordship and, when he died, stayed on.
Every morning here I have been surprised
By the stream that flows in the wrong direction.
I miss a mountain at the kitchen window.
The house is shrinking slowly to a few rooms
Where for longer periods she hides away
And sits arguing with herself, a hare
That chews over its droppings in the form.
I have caught her reading my letters home,
Hiding Christmas cards behind the piano.
She makes jokes to the friendly gardener
About my whiskery chin, my varicose veins,
And tells me off like a child in front of him
Should my fingernails be stained or floury.
If I start to talk about going home
She pretends not to understand my accent.
The bell that summons the afternoon tray
Will soon be ringing out for a bed pan.
Furniture and ornaments seem to linger
And wait under dust sheets for her to die.
A last sheet will cover up her armchair
And the hare that melts into the mountainside
Will be white in winter and eating snow.

I wanted to teach him the names of flowers,
Self-heal and centaury; on the long acre
Where cattle never graze, bog asphodel.
Could I love someone so gone in the head
And, as they say, was I leading him on?
He'd slept in the cot until he was twelve
Because of his babyish ways, I suppose,
Or the lack of a bed: hadn't his father
Gambled away all but rushy pasture?
His skull seemed to be hammered like a wedge
Into his shoulders, and his back was hunched,
Which gave him an almost scholarly air.
But he couldn't remember the things I taught:
Each name would hover above its flower
Like a butterfly unable to alight.
That day I pulled a cuckoo-pint apart
To release the giddy insects from their cell.
Gently he slipped his hand between my thighs.
I wasn't frightened; and still I don't know why,
But I ran from him in tears to tell them.
I heard how every day for one whole week
He was flogged with a blackthorn, then tethered
In the hayfield. I might have been the cow
Whose tail he would later dock with shears,
And he the ram tangled in barbed wire
That he stoned to death when they set him free.

Arrest

The sergeant called me by my christian name
And waited an hour while I tidied up.
Not once did he mention why he had come
Or when and where he would take me away.
He just moved quietly from wall to wall
As I swept the floor towards the flagstones
And leaned brush and shovel, the broken tongs
Next to the spade and hoe I'd brought inside.
I emptied the half-used packet of tea
Into the caddy and dusted the lid.
In the leaky basin with its brown ring
I washed knife, fork, spoon, the two teacups
And the saucer that does for an ashtray.
I put back the stools where they usually stand,
Hung the towel to dry over one of them
And spread fresh newspapers on the table.
When I'd thrown the water from the basin
I turned it upside down on the turf stack,
Then I packed my shaving brush and razor
And smoored the fire as though I might return.
They have locked me up in the institute
Because I made love to the animals.
I'd sooner stand barefoot, without a cap
And take in my acres from a distance,
From the rocky hilltops or the seashore,
From the purgatory of the windy gaps.

ENTOMOLOGY

I

A dinner service becoming mouths
With just one snorkel above the bog,
The sundew puts out roots into the air,
Improves its hungry house by taking in
Passers-by, midges, mayflies, prisoners
Digested by their handcuffs and chains.

II

To catch butterflies in a butterfly net
Is to sense the unfolding of a shroud,
Is to count the many changes of skin
And the chances of being born again,
Is to waken up after sleeping in.
Even their eggs are built with little doors.

BOTANY

Duckweed

Afloat on their own reflection, these leaves
With roots that reach only part of the way,
Will fall asleep at the end of summer,
Draw in their skirts and sink to the bottom.

Foxglove

Though the corolla dangles upside down,
Nothing ever falls out, neither nectar
Nor loosening pollen grains: a thimble,
Stall for the little finger and the bee.

Dock

Its green flowers attract only the wind
But a red vein may irrigate the leaf
And blossom into blush or birthmark
Or a remedy for the nettle's sting.

Orchid

The tuber absorbs summer and winter,
Its own ugly shape, twisted arms and legs,
A recollection of the heart, one artery
Sprouting upwards to support a flower.

BOG COTTON

Let me make room for bog cotton, a desert flower—
Keith Douglas, I nearly repeat what you were saying
When you apostrophised the poppies of Flanders
And the death of poetry there: that was in Egypt
Among the sandy soldiers of another war.

(It hangs on by a thread, denser than thistledown,
Reluctant to fly, a weather vane that traces
The flow of cloud shadow over monotonous bog—
And useless too, though it might well bring to mind
The plumpness of pillows, the staunching of wounds,

Rags torn from a petticoat and soaked in water
And tied to the bushes around some holy well
As though to make a hospital of the landscape—
Cures and medicines as far as the horizon
Which nobody harvests except with the eye.)

You saw that beyond the thirstier desert flowers
There fell hundreds of thousands of poppy petals
Magnified to blood stains by the middle distance
Or through the still unfocused sights of a rifle—
And Isaac Rosenberg wore one behind his ear.

THE WAR POETS

Unmarked were the bodies of the soldier-poets
For shrapnel opened up again the fontanel
Like a hailstone melting towards deep water
At the bottom of a well, or a mosquito
Balancing its tiny shadow above the lip.

It was rushes of air that took the breath away
As though curtains were drawn suddenly aside
And darkness streamed into the dormitory
Where everybody talked about the war ending
And always it would be the last week of the war.

PEACE
after Tibullus

Who was responsible for the very first arms deal—
The man of iron who thought of marketing the sword?
Or did he intend us to use it against wild animals
Rather than ourselves? Even if he's not guilty
Murder got into the bloodstream as gene or virus
So that now we give birth to wars, short cuts to death.
Blame the affluent society: no killings when
The cup on the dinner table was made of beechwood,
And no barricades or ghettos when the shepherd
Snoozed among sheep that weren't even thoroughbreds.

I would like to have been alive in the good old days
Before the horrors of modern warfare and warcries
Stepping up my pulse rate. Alas, as things turn out
I've been press-ganged into service, and for all I know
Someone's polishing a spear with my number on it.
God of my Fathers, look after me like a child!
And don't be embarrassed by this handmade statue
Carved out of bog oak by my great-great-grandfather
Before the mass-production of religious art
When a wooden god stood simply in a narrow shrine.

A man could worship there with bunches of early grapes,
A wreath of whiskery wheat-ears, and then say Thank you
With a wholemeal loaf delivered by him in person,
His daughter carrying the unbroken honeycomb.
If the good Lord keeps me out of the firing line
I'll pick a porker from the steamy sty and dress
In my Sunday best, a country cousin's sacrifice.
Someone else can slaughter enemy commanders
And, over a drink, rehearse with me his memoirs,
Mapping the camp in wine upon the table top.

It's crazy to beg black death to join the ranks
Who dogs our footsteps anyhow with silent feet—
No cornfields in Hell, nor cultivated vineyards,
Only yapping Cerberus and the unattractive
Oarsman of the Styx: there an anaemic crew
Sleepwalks with smoky hair and empty eye-sockets.
How much nicer to have a family and let
Lazy old age catch up on you in your retirement,
You keeping track of the sheep, your son of the lambs,
While the woman of the house puts on the kettle.

I want to live until the white hairs shine above
A pensioner's memories of better days. Meanwhile
I would like peace to be my partner on the farm,
Peace personified: oxen under the curved yoke;
Compost for the vines, grape-juice turning into wine,
Vintage years handed down from father to son;
Hoe and ploughshare gleaming, while in some dark corner
Rust keeps the soldier's grisly weapons in their place;
The labourer steering his wife and children home
In a hay cart from the fields, a trifle sozzled.

Then, if there are skirmishes, guerilla tactics,
It's only lovers quarrelling, the bedroom door
Wrenched off its hinges, a woman in hysterics,
Hair torn out, cheeks swollen with bruises and tears—
Until the bully-boy starts snivelling as well
In a pang of conscience for his battered wife:
Then sexual neurosis works them up again
And the row escalates into a war of words.
He's hard as nails, made of sticks and stones, the chap
Who beats his girlfriend up. A crime against nature.

Enough, surely, to rip from her skin the flimsiest
Of negligees, ruffle that elaborate hair-do,
Enough to be the involuntary cause of tears—
Though upsetting a sensitive girl when you sulk
Is a peculiar satisfaction. But punch-ups,
Physical violence, are out: you might as well
Pack your kit-bag, goose-step a thousand miles away
From the female sex. As for me, I want a woman
To come and fondle my ears of wheat and let apples
Overflow between her breasts. I shall call her Peace.

SULPICIA

Round this particular date I have drawn a circle
For Mars, dressed myself up for him, dressed to kill:
When I let my hair down I am a sheaf of wheat
And I bring in the harvest without cutting it.

Were he to hover above me like a bird of prey
I would lay my body out, his little country,
Fields smelling of flowers, flowers in the hedgerow—
And then I would put on an overcoat of snow.

I will stumble behind him through the undergrowth
Tracking his white legs, drawing about us both
The hunters' circle: among twisted nets and snares

I will seduce him, tangle his hairs with my hairs
While the stag dashes off on one of its tangents
And boars root safely along our circumference.

FLORENCE NIGHTINGALE

Through your pocket glass you have let disease expand
To remote continents of pain where you go far
With rustling cuff and starched apron, a soft hand:
Beneath the bandage maggots are stitching the scar.

For many of the men who lie there it is late
And you allow them at the edge of consciousness
The halo of your lamp, a brothel's fanlight
Or a nightlight carried in by nanny and nurse.

You know that even with officers and clergy
Moustachioed lips will purse into fundaments
And under sedation all the bad words emerge
To be rinsed in your head like the smell of wounds,

Death's vegetable sweetness at both rind and core—
Name a weed and you find it growing everywhere.

GRACE DARLING

After you had steered your coble out of the storm
And left the smaller islands to break the surface,
Like draughts shaking that colossal backcloth there came
Fifty pounds from the Queen, proposals of marriage.

The daughter of a lighthouse-keeper and the saints
Who once lived there on birds' eggs, rainwater, barley
And built to keep all pilgrims at a safe distance
Circular houses with views only of the sky,

Who set timber burning on the top of a tower
Before each was launched at last in his stone coffin—
You would turn your back on mainland and suitor
To marry, then bereave the waves from Lindisfarne,

A moth against the lamp that shines still and reveals
Many small boats at sea, lifeboats, named after girls.

METAMORPHOSES

I

A boulder locked in a cranny,
A head without a face, she waits
For rain to hollow out a font
And fill her eye in, blink by blink.

II

She will be felled like timber
So that anyone may study
Clefts made by the highest branches,
The faces hidden in the bark.

III

She sleeps in ponds and puddles
And sinks to her own level,
A bed for watercress, water
Snuggling in its own embrace.

IV

Her legs are the roots of a tree
That have grown around a boulder
As though she might give birth to it
By pressing hard into the ground.

MOUNTAIN SWIM

Hilltop and valley floor we sway between,
Our bodies sustained as by a hammock,
Our nakedness water stretched on stone,

One with the shepherd's distant whistle,
The hawk lifted on its thermal, the hare
Asleep in its excrement like a child.

MENISCUS

You are made out of water mostly, spittle, tears
And the blood that colours your cheek, red water.
Even your ears are ripples, your knuckles, knees
Damp stones that wear the meniscus like a skin.
Your breasts condense and adhere, drops of water.
And, where your body curves like a basin, faces
Are reflected, then dissolved by swaying water.

MARTINMAS

Not even ashes and the sweepings from the floor
Are to be thrown out, stray hairs of yours, flakes of skin,
For that would be digging a grave, burying someone
Before the weather mends and cold stones are lifted
From the river bed, the charred sticks from our hearth,
My sooty finger smudging your arm and forehead
As I leave to scatter grain into the furrows,
To wait with my sickle among the unripe stalks
Until the Feast of Saint Martin, you by my bed
Letting down your hair and weeping while you undress
Because you are the harvest I must gather in.
We grind the ears of corn to death between our bones.

ON MWEELREA

I

I was lowering my body on to yours
When I put my ear to the mountain's side
And eavesdropped on water washing itself
In the locked bath-house of the underground.

When I dipped my hand among hidden sounds
It was the water's pulse at wrist and groin,
It was the water that reminded me
To leave all of my jugs and cups behind.

II

The slopes of the mountain were commonage
For me clambering over the low walls
To look for the rings of autumn mushrooms
That ripple out across the centuries.

I had made myself the worried shepherd
Of snipe twisting the grasses into curls
And tiny thatches where they hid away,
Of the sheep that grazed your maidenhair.

III

September grew to shadows on Mweelrea
Once the lambs had descended from the ridge
With their fleeces dyed, tinges of sunset,
Rowan berries, and the bracken rusting.

Behind my eyelids I could just make out
In a wash of blood and light and water
Your body colouring the mountainside
Like uncut poppies in the stubbly fields.

THE LINEN INDUSTRY

Pulling up flax after the blue flowers have fallen
And laying our handfuls in the peaty water
To rot those grasses to the bone, or building stooks
That recall the skirts of an invisible dancer,

We become a part of the linen industry
And follow its processes to the grubby town
Where fields are compacted into window-boxes
And there is little room among the big machines.

But even in our attic under the skylight
We make love on a bleach green, the whole meadow
Draped with material turning white in the sun
As though snow reluctant to melt were our attire.

What's passion but a battering of stubborn stalks,
Then a gentle combing out of fibres like hair
And a weaving of these into christening robes,
Into garments for a marriage or funeral?

Since it's like a bereavement once the labour's done
To find ourselves last workers in a dying trade,
Let flax be our matchmaker, our undertaker,
The provider of sheets for whatever the bed—

And be shy of your breasts in the presence of death,
Say that you look more beautiful in linen
Wearing white petticoats, the bow on your bodice
A butterfly attending the embroidered flowers.

HOUSEHOLD HINTS

Old clothes have hearts, livers that last longer:
The veils, chemises, embroidered blouses
Brought back to life in suds and warm water,
Black lace revived by black tea, or crape
Passed to and fro through steam from a kettle.

So look on this as an antique nightdress
That has sleepwalked along hundreds of miles
Of rugs and carpets and linoleum,
Its clean hem lifted over the spilt milk
And ink, the occasional fall of soot.

This places you at a dressing-table,
Two sleeves that float into the looking-glass
Above combs and brushes, mother-of-pearl,
Tortoiseshell, silver, the discreet litter
Of your curling papers and crimping pins.

Though I picked it up for next to nothing
Wear this each night against your skin, accept
My advice about blood stains and mildew,
Cedar wood and camphor as protection
Against moths, alum-water against fire,

For I have been bruised like the furniture
And am more than a list of household hints,
The blackleader of stoves and bootscrapers,
Mender of sash cords, the mirror you slip
Between sheets to prove that the bed is damp.

DEAD MEN'S FINGERS

The second time we meet I am waiting in a pub
Beside the cigarette machine. She is in her moons.
A cat with a mouse's tail dangling out of its mouth
Flashes from between her legs and escapes into my head.
There follow trips to the seaside where I find for her
Feathers, shells, dune violets among the marram grass;

Then the conversational strolls in a forest of pines
So that I can picture the invisible tree-creeper
Spiralling up her body to probe for such parasites
As lurk where pink flowers seem to harden into cones.
Next comes that honeymoon weekend in a farflung cottage
Where we sit in silence and borrow light from the door,

And I boil a somnolent lobster in the ash bucket
And divide it between us. Our most memorable meal.
But surely she has eaten dead men's fingers by mistake
Because her sickness interrupts us like a telephone.
The tenth, eleventh, twelfth occasions melt together
Colourfully: a stained-glass window in a burning church.

Indeed, I soon find myself, wherever a fire is lit,
Crossing my legs, putting my feet up on the mantelpiece
And talking to my shoes, with glances in her direction.
The first time we meet is really the last time in reverse.
We kiss for ever and I feel like the ghost of a child
Visiting the mother who long ago aborted him.

THE BARBER'S WIFE

I seem to be the last customer
For blinds are drawn on instruments,

On combs and razors, clicking scissors,
Clippers that buzz among pomades.

As though everything depends on it
A drop of water clings to the tap,

A lens inverting the premises
Until the barber's wife appears.

Does she always come at five o'clock
To sweep the presences, absences,

Earthly remains, ghosts of skulls
With graceful movements into the bin?

She is an interloper, two eyes
Penetrating the back of my head.

Then I see that she repeats herself
In one mirror after another,

That the barber and I are eunuchs
In the harem of her reflections.

SELF-PORTRAIT

My great-great-grandfather fell in top hat and tails
Across the threshold, his cigar brightly burning
While the chalk outline they had traced around his body
Got up and strolled through the door and became me,

But not before his own son had wasted a lifetime
Waiting to be made Lord Mayor of the Universe.
He was to choke to death on a difficult word
When a food particle lodged against his uvula.

I came into being alongside a twin brother
Who threatened me at first like an abortionist
Recommending suicide jumps and gin with cloves.
Then he blossomed into my guardian angel.

Peering back to the people who ploughed the Long Field
My eyes are bog holes that reflect a foreign sky.
Moustaches thatch my utterance in such a way
That no one can lipread the words from a distance.

I am, you will have noticed, all fingers and thumbs
But, then, so is the wing of a bat, a bird's wing.
I articulate through the nightingale's throat,
Sing with the vocal chords of the orang-outang.

CODICILS

I

Your hands hold my neck and head
As though you were bathing me
Or lifting me out of darkness,
Hands that shelter a night-light,
Balance a spoon for medicine.

When you turn from me to sleep
A lamplighter on his bicycle
Will see you to the corner,
Gas mantles in his saddle bag,
Across his shoulder a long pole.

II

It is a last desolate weaning
When you hug me, the sole survivor
—Without location or protocol—
Of a tribe which let the fire go out.

I shall explain to the first stranger
With a smattering of my dialect
Why I am huddled up in mourning
And, like a baby, sucking my thumb.

V

NEW POEMS

I have been tapping the distances between us,
An engineer at his ease up a telegraph pole
Or a saboteur galvanized on the power lines,
Wedding ring and buttons soldered to his skin.

VIEW

I have put my arms around her skeleton
For fear that her forearms might unravel
Like hawsers, ligaments stiffening to kelp
That keeps ocean and boulders in their places,
Weights on the heart, ballast for the ribcage,
Stones to be lifted out of the currach
And arranged as a sundial where she points
To the same cottage on every island—
There's always a view over her shoulder.

PATCHWORK

I

There are ribbons that hold you together,
Hooks and eyes, hollows at the collarbone,

As though you dismantle your skeleton
Before stepping out of the crumpled ring,

Your nipples under my fingertips
Like white flowers on a white ground.

II

I pull up over us old clothes, remnants,
Stitching together shirts and nightshirts

Into such a dazzle as will burn away
Newspapers, letters, previous templates,

The hearth too, a red patch at the centre
That scorches the walls and our low ceiling.

I

Come hugging your breasts
As if to comfort them,
Ripening in your armpit
Fingertip, knuckle-bone
And then, like a branch,
Canopy the windfalls.

II

You will reduce me to an eel
That drenches the stubble, inhales
The dew, a thorn in a puddle
Dimpling the water's membrane.

III

My shadow covers you,
The foxglove or harebell
Where insects go to sleep,
Or the pimpernel
That closes for a cloud.

IV

Implicate in your hair
Timorous featherbrains,
Headaches in the hedge,
Eggs warming and cooling
On cobwebs, thistledown,
White ones you pluck out.

You have collected me into your hand
Now that the blackbird abandons the nest,
Yolks curdling beneath their porcelain,

A grave in the branches for wind and weeds
To cover up, and not the mother's breast,
The teepee she makes of bones and feathers.

VI

When your hair covers my eyes
My hand behaves like the wind
That parts a cornfield to expose
Cornflowers drowning, one poppy
With petals crinkled and hot.

VII

From my belly or thigh
As love evaporates,
Lift with your fingernail
A flake of rice-paper,

Weigh what meat there is
On the shin of a wren,
The marrow full of air,
The feathers full of rain.

VIII

My mouth reads into you
Light behind the rain,
Boulders beneath the soil,
Between breath and bone
Water gone underground.

IX

Where barley weighs the food in its hair
You materialise like a farmer's wife
Who last summer occupied the distance
—A sewing basket among the stooks—
And left me behind, trawling the milk
With goose-grass for strands of your hair.

X

Some parts of the body
Must part from it, making
A wake-house out of you,

Out of my arrivals
A perpetual mourning
At all the lucky doors.

XI

You leave a moon at the window
And, as the lifeless nebulae
Sink beneath my sleeping hand,
Not one red vein in the sky.

MAGGIE MOORE'S

I am standing behind you in Maggie Moore's
Second-hand clothes shop in Sandy Row.
A single electric light bulb
Raises the bumps on the bumpy floor.
You rummage through crochet-work and cobwebs.

Moths flit out from the sweaty arm-holes
Of party frocks and summer dresses,
Nightdresses mothers and grandmothers wore.
As in a dream all take off their clothes
And vanish for ever down Sandy Row.

I am the guard who polishes his rifle
With a rag you recognise as silk
Or chiffon, perfect material
For you to embroider with designs
That cover and reveal your body.

And I am the young amazed G.I.
Passing rag after rag through barbed wire
And ripping the sleeve of his uniform.
He knows that your clothes are second-hand.
He brings down the shutters on Maggie Moore's.

LOVE POEM

When my fingers touch your body's
Sorrowing stubble, so young
You feel, so old, all I can see
Is an area with barbed wire
And an orphan squatting there.

It is nineteen forty, forty-one
Which makes him a sort of twin,
But he has never known a tree
And he does not laugh or cry
Or wait for your hairs to grow.

LOVE POET

I make my peace with murderers.
I lock pubic hair from victims
In an airtight tin, mummify
Angel feathers, tobacco shreds.

All that survives my acid bath
Is a solitary gall-stone
Like a pebble out on mud flats
Or the ghost of an avocado.

AMONG WATERBIRDS

Between us and the wind from the wetlands
There are no windbreaks but waterbirds' wings.

A duck egg balances, greeny-blue,
And eclipses the feathers of the sun.

You are my weather-sense, crests lifting—
Let me use your body like a hide.

MARKINGS
for Sarah

I

The markings almost disappear
With the shadowy sound you make
Launching the feather from your hand,
As though you would learn to whistle
By answering the curlew's cry.

II

I would remember tumblers
Above the water-meadow,
The shimmer of white feathers
In the flower-dwarfing wind,

Brood-patch and bird-brain,
The hummock of her body
That tries to make head or tail
Of movements inside the shell.

All that remains to show you
Is the deserted nest-bowl,
Blots and scribbles on an egg,
The dappled flight of lapwings.

III

One more pebble on the cairn
Might make it a vantage point
For the stonechat, a headstone
Should winter blow out his song,
His chestnut breast a tinderbox
Igniting the few syllables.

HALLOWE'EN

It is Hallowe'en. Turnip Head
Will soon be given his face,
A slit, two triangles, a hole.
His brains litter the table top.
A candle stub will be his soul.

SMOKE IN THE BRANCHES

The Disfigurement of Fergus

This is a scream no one will have heard
Bubbling up out of his mind, nightmare
Distorting his face on the sea-bed
To an ugliness that craves its mirror,
A watery death to cure and wash
The King of Ulster and his blemish.

The Grey of Macha

When big tears of blood roll down the face
Of the Grey of Macha, Cuchulain's horse,
They sprinkle the chariot and harness
That might as well be dragging a hearse
Over a battlefield slushy with brains,
Over the teeth like a shower of hailstones.

The Bewilderment of Muircertach

Muircertach mac Erca, King of Ireland,
Is waging war against fern and thistle,
Damaging pebbles, wounding the ground
Between life and death, grave and castle,
Where the woman he adores will vanish
Like a puffball or smoke in the branches.

The Death of Mac Glas

He isn't pulling a funny face
Although the Leinstermen laugh at him
Who, seconds ago, was only Mac Glas
The jester contriving another game,
While the entrails, tugged by a raven
Out of his wound, loop up to heaven.

ON SLIEVE GULLION
for Douglas Carson

On Slieve Gullion 'men and mountain meet',
O'Hanlon's territory, the rapparee,
Home of gods, backdrop for a cattle raid,
The Lake of Cailleach Beara at the top
That slaked the severed head of Conor Mor:

To the south the Border and Ravensdale
Where the torturers of Nairac left
Not even an eyelash under the leaves
Or a tooth for MacCecht the cupbearer
To rinse, then wonder where the water went.

I watch now through a gap in the hazels
A blackened face, the disembodied head
Of a mummer who has lost his bearings
Or, from the garrison at Dromintee,
A paratrooper on reconnaissance.

He draws a helicopter after him,
His beret far below, a wine-red spot
Swallowed by heathery patches and ling
As he sweats up the slopes of Slieve Gullion
With forty pounds of history on his back.

Both strangers here, we pass in silence
For he and I have dried the lakes and streams
And Conor said too long ago: 'Noble
And valiant is MacCecht the cupbearer
Who brings water that a king may drink.'

NO MAN'S LAND
in memory of Isaac Rosenberg

I

Who will give skin and bones to my Jewish granny?
She has come down to me in the copperplate writing
Of three certificates, a dog-eared daguerreotype
And the one story my grandfather told about her.

He tossed a brick through a rowdy neighbour's window
As she lay dying, and Jessica, her twenty years
And mislaid whereabouts gave way to a second wife,
A terrible century, a circle of christian names.

II

I tilt her head towards you, Isaac Rosenberg,
But can you pick out that echo of splintering glass
From under the bombardment, and in No Man's Land
What is there to talk about but difficult poems?

Because your body was not recovered either
I try to read the constellations of brass buttons,
Identity discs that catch the light a little.
A shell-shocked carrier pigeon flaps behind the lines.

THE THIRD LIGHT

The sexton is opening up the grave,
Lining with mossy cushions and couch grass
This shaft of light, entrance to the earth
Where I kneel to marry you again,
My elbows in darkness as I explore
From my draughty attic your last bedroom.
Then I vanish into the roof space.

I have handed over to him your pain
And your preference for Cyprus sherry,
Your spry quotations from the *Daily Mail*
With its crossword solved in ink, your limp
And pills, your scatter of cigarette butts
And last-minute humorous spring-cleaning
Of one corner of a shelf in his cupboard.

You spent his medals like a currency,
Always refusing the third light, afraid
Of the snipers who would extinguish it.
Waiting to scramble hand in hand with him
Out of the shell hole, did you imagine
A Woodbine passing to and fro, a face
That stabilises like a smoke ring?

THE WHITE BUTTERFLY

I wish that before you died
I had told you the legend,
A story from the Blaskets
About how the cabbage-white
May become the soul of one
Who lies sleeping in the fields.

Out of his mouth it wanders
And in through the eye-socket
Of an old horse's skull
To explore the corridors
And empty chamber, then
Flies back inside his lips.

This is a dream and flowers
Are bordering the journey
And the road leads on towards
That incandescent palace
Where from one room to the next
There is no one to be seen.

When I asked you as a child
How high should fences be
To keep in the butterflies,
Blood was already passing
Down median and margin
To the apex of a wing.

RUNE

Poems in the palm of the hand, life-lines,
Fingers tapping the ridge of the shin-bone,
The bridge of the nose, fingerprints, breath;
Then the silvery skin of the lifeless,
Ivy increasing the secrets, the answers—
The physician's power in cold dwellings,
Candles behind this veil of synonyms,
A blind man's lovely wife and signature.

parce tamen, per te furtivi foedera lecti,
per venerem quaeso compositumque caput . . .

p. 51: A freemartin is a heifer whose hormones have been overwhelmed in the womb by those of her male twin. She is born sterile and, sometimes, sexually malformed.

p. 75: The stories referred to are Kingsley's *The Water Babies* and Andersen's *The Snow Queen*.

p. 80: The Moebius Band or Strip is an example of a non-orientable surface. It can be illustrated by taking a strip of paper several times longer than it is wide and sticking the two ends together after twisting one of them by a half turn. It is one-sided in the sense that an ant could crawl along the whole length of the strip without crossing the bounding edge and find itself at the starting point on 'the other side'.

p. 85: The Act of Union between Ireland and England became operative in 1801. Positions of privilege granted to those who acquiesced in this are sometimes called Union Titles.

p. 95: The Irish painter Gerard Dillon was born in the Lower Falls district of Belfast in 1916. He died in 1971.

p. 119: A *bullaun* is a square or cylindrical block of granite into which a deep hole has been cut to make a roughly shaped stone basin.

p. 124: A *fleadh* is a festival of traditional Irish music, a *bodhran* a goatskin drum.

p. 146: Oliver Plunkett's mummified head is kept in a glass casket on an altar in Drogheda Cathedral.

p. 160: The Echo Gate is situated on the outskirts of Trim in County Meath.

p. 167: The poems alluded to are *Desert Flowers* by Keith Douglas and Isaac Rosenberg's *Break of Day in the Trenches*.

p. 172: Sulpicia was a Roman poet of the Augustan age. This sonnet is a collage of original lines and free translations of lines and phrases from the Latin.

p. 174: A coble is a Northumbrian fishing-boat.

p. 181: Dead men's fingers, the lungs of a lobster, are inedible.

p. 197: *Muircertach* is dissyllabic and could be anglicised as *Murtagh*.

p. 198: Robert Nairac, officially described as an 'undercover liaison officer' between the army and the police, disappeared in May 1977. The search for him was concentrated on Ravensvale Forest. His body has yet to be found.